Skulking in the Woods

IRREGULAR WARFARE IN PENNSYLVANIA DURING THE SEVEN YEARS' WAR

Ben Scharff

HERITAGE BOOKS
2014

HERITAGE BOOKS

AN IMPRINT OF HERITAGE BOOKS, INC.

Books, CDs, and more—Worldwide

For our listing of thousands of titles see our website
at
www.HeritageBooks.com

Published 2014 by
HERITAGE BOOKS, INC.
Publishing Division
5810 Ruatan Street
Berwyn Heights, Md. 20740

International Standard Book Numbers
Paperbound: 978-0-7884-3708-3
Clothbound: 978-0-7884-8113-0

To my mother

iv

TABLE OF CONTENTS

MAPS

PREFACE

This project has taken a winding road to reach press.

Originally conceptualized and produced as my Master's thesis at

Slippery Rock University in 2006, I prepared it for publication in

2007. As often happens with such projects, various circumstances

conspired to delay its arrival until now. As also happens, the

intervening years have provided further insights that suggest

updates were in order. After rereading the manuscript, however, I

opted to leave it as it was originally written.

History is a magical thing, possessing the power to fire the

imagination. For some of us, this develops into an all-

encompassing passion that that we devote our careers to

discovering its truths. My own deep fascination with the past

reaches back to my earliest memories when my father took my

three brothers and myself (usually to give my mother a reprieve)

to a variety of historical sites in northwest Ohio. Rereading this

manuscript reminded me of that child-like wonder because it

brings to life an inherently entertaining narrative. At the same time, this narrative puts forth an important argument that still passes muster a decade after its original conception.

I was also inspired to maintain the manuscript in its original form due to the fond memories I have of those who contributed to its production, too many of whom are gone. My original acknowledgments addressed the loss of my mother and David Dixon, my advisor and mentor at Slippery Rock. Since then, two additional contributors—Joe McDermott and Willam Pencak—have likewise left us too early. This draft thus serves as a means of commemorating those two excellent scholars whose influence was critical. Not all has been sadness, however, and many individuals have joined Dave, Joe and Bill as influences on my work. Dan Barr, another former protégé of Dave's, has emerged as an excellent friend and mentor along with Tyler Boulware who guided me through my doctoral work. I have now embarked on the next stage of my career as a faculty member of the history department at Mercyhurst University and have already benefitted from association with my new colleagues, several of whom have xi

already provided me with useful advice and suggestions. And

Shasta, of course, has given my life greater purpose. This book

thus represents the bridge between two very different periods in

my life and I have enjoyed revisiting them in the form of this

manuscript. I sincerely hope the reader finds it both entertaining

and informative.

Benjamin G. Scharff

Mercyhurst University, 2014

ACKNOWLEDGEMENTS

Many people are deserving of thanks for the completion of my work. Friends David Antoline and Tim Kushon sat down with me and provided crucial assistance in formatting the text...help that saved me countless hours of frustration. Colleagues and friends Jim McKee, Travis Bercel, and Joe McDermott frequently discussed the project with me and helped me refine my work. Dr. Bill Pencak at The Pennsylvania State University and Dr. Daniel Barr at Robert Morris University both read my completed work and provided insightful comments. Andrew Knez Jr., a fine traditional artist and friend, was kind enough to offer the use of his artwork for the book. Friend and colleague Jason Espino deserves special thanks for spending many painstaking hours producing the very accurate maps shown throughout the book. Finally, thanks are deserving of the history department faculty at Slippery Rock University where I was attending graduate school as I worked on the project. They provided me with the skills and direction needed to complete the work. Special thanks go to Dr. David Dixon, who advised me throughout the process and certainly had more of an effect on the outcome than any other individual. It is with great sadness that David will not see the finished product, but his legacy is stamped on this humble attempt to replicate his ability as a historian.

My family put up with me the entire way. My brothers, Andy and Pete Scharff, constantly checked on my progress. My dad and brother Jon Scharff, gave me all the space I needed. Finally, most of all, I have to thank my mother. Without the importance she placed on education, I would not have even begun the project. She will never get to read my work, but she did have the opportunity to see where I was headed. For that, I am grateful. People told me along the way how impressed they were that I could stay focused in the wake of her passing. I always responded that I could focus specifically because I wanted to make her proud. For that reason, I dedicate this entire book to her memory.

INTRODUCTION

Less than a decade after France and Great Britain last battled in North America, tensions once again mounted in 1753. This time, the friction resulted from competing claims to the Ohio country–the land now encompassed by Western Pennsylvania. During the winter of 1753-1754, Virginia Governor Robert Dinwiddie dispatched young Major George Washington in company with the intrepid frontiersmen Christopher Gist, interpreter Jacob Van Braam, and several other men to warn French encroachers off what Dinwiddie considered Virginian, and hence British, territory. After politely caring for Washington's tired and haggard winter party, the French declined to leave. Thus began the string of events that led to war in the Ohio country.

During the resulting campaigns, Indian and European irregular warriors joined with more traditional French and British soldiers to wage battle in which both sides experienced victories and defeats. Folk history, television, films, and literature often glamorize the contributions of heroic and independent irregular-type soldiers. At the same time, regular troops, while disciplined, often appear completely ineffective and out of their element. Irregulars almost always prevail over them.

The design and tactics employed by regular forces indeed suited them for combat in open areas. These tactics, however, did not automatically make them unsuited for conflicts within forested areas. Also, while irregular tactics exploited the opportunities allowed in the cover of the woods, they did not have an overwhelming effect on the outcomes of battles and in the ultimate decision of victory or defeat. Instead of simply concluding that irregulars exhibited more effectiveness in the woods than regulars because they hid behind trees and took careful aim while regulars stood in the open in massed ranks, battles and campaigns must be analyzed in a broader context. Discipline, experience, leadership, decision-making, pure luck, and overall strategy must be considered. The following chapters strive to illuminate these factors in individual battles and campaigns, and determine the actual contribution of irregular warriors, and whether regulars could indeed hold their own in wilderness conflicts.

Chapter one attempts to lay the necessary groundwork for subsequent chapters. It focuses on the vegetation, terrain, and waterways that covered the area in which irregular and regular forces traveled and fought in the Ohio country. It then proceeds to outline the various types of irregular warriors that France and Britain recruited to complement their regular armies. Finally, the chapter suggests the differing strategies of the warring nations and how those affected the use, importance, and success of irregular troops.

Chapter two considers the causes of Washington's defeat at Fort Necessity. Lack of irregulars in his force, poor decision making, lack of discipline and experience, and simple overwhelming numbers played a role.

Chapter three analyzes General Edward Braddock's defeat at the Monongahela. Many of the same considerations apply. Factors include the absence of irregulars amongst the British,

Braddock's order of march, and the discipline and experience of his soldiers.

Chapter four examines the intervening years of 1756 and 1757 when Britain failed to launch campaigns in the southern theater. Pennsylvania, left to its own devices, employed a variety of techniques to beat back the irregular raids of the French and their Indian allies. Typically, the results proved disappointing. The consequences were not always the result of superior tactics, other factors also contributed.

Chapter five discusses the final British victory over the French in the region during General John Forbes's expedition. Reasons why Forbes had been successful where Washington and Braddock had not need illumination. An examination of Forbes's winning formula, whether he utilized irregular tactics better than his predecessors or merely adapted regular techniques, becomes critical.

Chapter six concludes with an analysis of Colonel Henry Bouquet's unprecedented triumph over the Indians at Bushy Run.

Discussion revolves around how, with a force almost entirely composed of regulars, was the colonel able to defeat a determined army of Indians using presumably superior tactics. The results of the chapters may be surprising. While superior tactics certainly gave combatants that utilized them an advantage, other factors such as discipline, leadership, and decision-making proved every bit as important. With the examination of each campaign and battle in detail, it appears apparent that while irregulars certainly performed a crucial role in the conflict as a whole, their myth of superiority fades.

CHAPTER 1

"An Immense Uninhabited Wilderness"

An eighteenth century army seeking to operate in the wild region of the Ohio Country faced innumerable challenges. From the deep forests to the treacherous waterways, from the endless mountain ridges to the frustrating roadways, every movement presented a new obstacle. European officers found themselves far from the pleasant campaigning fields of Europe, and often turned to non-traditional troops to overcome these obstacles. French officers and leaders could rely upon woods-wise French colonists, while the British often looked towards their own inexperienced North American citizens. Both sides, to different degrees of success, courted ideally suited Indian warriors. These three distinct groups of irregular troops provided the road building, convoy protection, and intelligence needs of both the French and British armies. They also made various contributions in combat. Irregular soldiers thus represented the means, whether successfully or not, with which the European officers attempted to overcome the unique difficulties of warfare in the Ohio Country. In the end, however, the skill of the respective irregular warriors, and the different objectives and strategies of the two nations, determined the effectiveness of such units.

To the European eye, the Ohio Country in the mid-eighteenth century sometimes seemed "an immense uninhabited Wilderness overgrown everywhere with trees and underbrush."[1] To the savvy colonist, that same land could be described as wanting "[n]othing but Cultivation to make it a most delightfull Country."[2] In fact, place names—Great Meadows, Laurel Mountain, Chestnut Ridge, Le Boeuf Creek—and contemporary accounts suggest a wide variety of vegetation, wildlife, and terrain. Large hardwoods and occasional stands of pines infested the rolling landscape. Maple, crab apple, cherry, and mulberry trees provided wild foodstuffs for the knowledgeable inhabitant.[3] The forests were often so thick that, according to Bishop Spangenburg, "one does not see the sun all day long."[4] In many areas, the forest grew so thick that native inhabitants burned forests to promote undergrowth favored by wild game.[5] In many areas of the Ohio Country, therefore, low levels of underbrush and widely spaced trees did not present much of an impediment for eighteenth century armies.

On fewer occasions, however, vegetation could be troublesome. In the early 1750s, Christopher Gist noted areas "bushy and very full of Thorns."[6] Some hillsides, heavily covered in laurel thickets, became impassable. Finally, deadfalls posed a constant nuisance, especially when armies began the process of road building. Tree stumps could create a problem during the construction of roads, though the largeness of the tree growth often left wide-open spaces on the forest floor.[7] Vegetation created difficult areas, but they remained infrequent. Forest growth itself thus did not typically pose an impediment to the progress of an eighteenth century army.

While vegetation alone did not typically deter the movements of armies, neither did it aid the process. The general lack of underbrush and open meadows forced most campaigners to carry fodder for draft animals and thus strained the already

precarious supply lines. The lack of cultivated plants and

difficulty of feeding large numbers of men through hunting and

gathering further exacerbated supply difficulties. The inhospitality

of the forest to colonists and Europeans unknowledgeable in

woodcraft proved an impediment in itself.[8]

A true physical barrier did lie between eighteenth century

armies and the Ohio Country. A vast and complicated series of

parallel ridges and valleys, the Appalachian Mountains at times

became known simply as the "endless mountains". Sometimes the

ridges remained quite near to each other. At other times, as much

as twenty miles separated them with smaller ridges within the

valleys themselves. In the east, the mountains began rather

abruptly, quickly rising a thousand feet. In the west, however, the

three final ridges—Allegheny Mountain, Chestnut Ridge, and

Laurel Ridge—marked the beginning of a gradual descent towards

the westward. The ground here undulated still.[9] In his travels in

the early 1750s for the Ohio Company, Gist noted, "after you are past the Allegheny Mountain, the Ground is rough in many

Places."[10] In these seemingly endless barriers, eighteenth century

armies encountered the greatest difficulty in movement.

The extreme vastness of the territory compounded the

problems caused by the actual roughness of the terrain. While

trying to stake out a route for the army of General Edward

Braddock, Sir Jon St. Clair lamented, "no one except a few

Hunters knows it [the land] on the Spot; and their knowledge

extends no further than in following their Game."[11] Picking easy,

level ground proved worthless if it only led to rougher country.

Whereas, taking a slightly more difficult path might prove

beneficial if it led to better land further down the road. It became

essential, therefore, for road builders to possess accurate

intelligence of the mountainous terrain, which often proved

difficult. The breaks in the Appalachian chain—the West Branch

of the Susquehanna River, the Juniata River, and the Monongahela

River water route from the southeast—seemed the solution to the

uninformed planner.[12]

Although the water routes from the east ultimately proved inefficient or worse, the Monongahela River received special interest early from English colonists. A young George Washington reported in 1753 that it appeared "deep and still, without any perceptible Fall."[13] Back in 1754 at the head of an army near the Youghiogeny River, Washington wrote Governor Dinwiddie that "[t]hese Indians, and all the Traders that I have been able to get any information from…assure me, that (except one place) Water Carriage may be had down this River."[14] One military planner further estimated that using the Potomac, Youghiogheny, and Monongahela Rivers left only 114 land miles to be traveled to the Ohio River from the inhabited regions of the colonies. Unfortunately, however, the situation on the Monongahela and its tributaries, as well as on most rivers, proved unfavorable for the transportation of large military bodies.[15]

Although the French generally possessed better water routes from the north using French Creek and the Allegheny River from the Great Lakes, they too remained subject to the whims of nature. Often, the water froze in the winter.[16] On November 21, 1752, Christopher Gist had forsaken water travel in the winter because he found "ice...so hard we could not break our way through."[17] Sometimes, "water...was frozen hard enough for us to pass over on the ice."[18] Surely then, aquatic movement in the winter represented an undependable mode of transportation, and other seasons brought additional difficulties.

The waterways of the Ohio Country at times became extremely shallow. During Braddock's campaign, George Washington took solace in the fact that "[French] reinf'ts...cou'd not arrive with Pro'vns or any Supplies dur'g the continuance of the Droughth as the Buffalo River...must be as Dry as we now f'd the g't xing of the Youghe., w'ch may be pass'd dry shod."[19] When the English reached the Monongahela River, the troops found "[t]he River is betwixt two and three hundred yards Over and not much more than knee deep."[20] Thus, in the seasons when eighteenth century armies did not find the rivers frozen, they often found them too shallow for transport of heavy loads. Even when water levels reached higher levels, however, one final obstacle

remained.[21]

Peaceful boating down waterways, with pleasant forested

banks and manageable still waters, could become troublesome in a

hurry. Travelers might come "to a fall, which continued rough,

rocky, and scarcely passable, for two miles, and then fell, within

the space of fifty yards, nearly forty feet perpendicular."[22] Even

with this grim reality, optimism generally prevailed in the early

1750s until the true situation of many rivers and streams became

apparent. One British official, with the complacency of one

judging conditions from afar, explained, "[e]xcept these [falls] &

the Temporary Rapidity arising from the Frestes of Spring & the

Rainy Seasons all the Waters of the Messesippi run to the Ocean

with a Still, Easy & Gentle current." Even Washington, much

closer to scene of action, underestimated the difficulty arising

from rough waters. On May 18, 1754, he set out by canoe to

reconnoiter the Youghiogheny River. He set out in high hopes,

and returned five days later knowing that the river would never be passable. Dreams of a water route from the southeast finally died.

With the seasonal difficulties of ice and drought and the year-

round danger of rough waters and falls, the English, and to a lesser

degree the French, all too often came to rely upon roads to

navigate to the Ohio Country.[23]

When builders set out to construct roads, they often found

preexisting Indian paths a convenient guide for their work. Long

before the arrival of any European, routes of trade and

communication linked the people of the continent. The paths

typically treaded the best land, following well-drained uplands and

avoiding damper areas. Well-traveled paths usually remained

broad and clear all year round. Getting lost was common, but only

because the abundance of routes sometimes created confusion.[24]

General John Forbes, during his 1758 campaign, acknowledged

the aid his army received from following Indian paths. He wrote

Secretary of State William Pitt, "the whole being an immense

Forest of 240 miles of Extant, intersected by several ranges of

Mountains, impenetrable almost to any thing humane save the

Indians, (if they be allowed the Appellation) who have foot paths, or tracts through those desarts, by the help of which, we make our roads."[25] The Indians, however, did not design roads to support wagons and massive amounts of traffic at once.

Roads required tremendous efforts to build, and even despite massive amounts of work, ambitious campaigners could still be frustrated by the intervention of nature. St. Clair, charged with building a road for Braddock in 1755, noted, "[t]he Roads are either Rocky or full of Bogs, we are obliged to blow the Rocks and lay Bridges every day."[26] Trees had to be cut down, and stumps needed either removed or sheered close enough to the ground that wagons could pass over them. Such efforts might be undermined by something as simple as several rainy days, as Forbes found out in 1758. He wrote his subordinate, Colonel Henry Bouquet, "a few Dry days would make things wear a more favorable aspect as all Clay Countrys are either good or bad for Carriages according to the wett or dry season."[27] Beyond these difficulties, road builders needed the trained eye of a surveyor to negotiate the tricky grades

of a hill country.

To chose the correct paths, engineers also needed to know

what lay beyond the next hill. Such information could be nearly

impossible to obtain. Hoping to rely upon local informants,

Braddock eventually realized his colonial cousins had sorely

misinformed him. Writing to England on June 8, 1755, he raged,

"[t]his part of the Country is absolutely unknown to the

Inhabitants of the lower parts of Virginia and Maryland, their

Account of the Roads...utterly false."[28] Due to the general's

failure to extract accurate information from the provincials,

intelligence needed gathered. That too, however, proved difficult

as St. Clair found out. He lamented, "[i]t is certain that the ground

is not easy to be reconnoitered for one may go twenty Miles

without seeing before him ten yards."[29] To gain this and other

necessary intelligence, as well as to build and keep up the roads,

protect convoys, and assist in military action, both France and

England turned to irregular warriors already in North America.

They found recruits among their own colonists and in the various Indian nations living in the forest.

On paper, Britain appeared to possess incredible advantages in material and manpower over France. With an advantage in colonial manpower as large as twenty to one, the British should have been able to overwhelm the French at will. The intangibles, however, favored France. While the British provincials tended to be farmers and tradesmen unskilled in wilderness ways and war, many Canadians had been trained in the forest through experience in the fur trade. Furthermore, while British colonists possessed a tendency to be locally interested and resentful of authority, Canadians typically shared a unity of purpose. These various attributes helped even the score between the two warring empires.[30]

The unity of purpose with which the French fought the English resulted from strong governmental control. The *London Magazine* noted, "the Tenants…are thereby obliged, on any Occasion, to take up Arms for their Defence."[31] The Canadians apparently served in this capacity without argument. The *London Magazine* further proclaimed that, "[t]he whole [Canada] being likewise under one general Command, the People obey with such Alacrity, That (to use the Words of a Memorial before me) in Case of any Attack, they all fly, on the first Notice, to the Place of Danger, as readily as in a Garrison on beating or sounding a Call."[32] In addition to enthusiasm, these troops possessed relatively high levels of experience. The government of Canada took great pains to train their people in warfare. To further this training, officials encouraged Canadians to take tours of the lakes to gain knowledge in the wilderness. In fact, military commissions often remained unavailable to those who had not taken such a tour. Lower class citizens received approval from French leaders for marrying into Indian tribes. There, they could teach their children to hunt and live in the Indian ways. For these reasons, the Canadian government groomed a large cadre of experienced citizen-soldiers.[33]

Many Canadians appeared all too happy to take up the Indian way of life. Father Charlevoix, a Jesuit priest, described this willingness. He observed "the attraction which the young men feel to this savage way of life which consists of doing nothing, in being restrained by nothing, in pursueing all one's urges, and placing oneself beyond the possibility of correction."[34] During the process of adoption, many Canadians gained knowledge of canoes, snowshoes, native languages, and other various aspects of Indian culture.[35] In fact, the *London Magazine* claimed that Canadians "so naturally conform themselves to the Indian Ways, as scarce to be distinguished."[36] Despite objections from some such as Charlevoix, the ability to cross cultural lines, and the skills gained from such experience, proved beneficial to the government of Canada in wartime.

The English became well aware of the benefits such a system afforded the French. The *Maryland Gazette* explained, "[b]y these Means, they are early inured to Toil and Fatigue, learn all the stratagems practiced in their Method of warring, and imbibe the same cruel and ferocious Disposition."[37] Many considered the

Canadians equal to the Indians in the woods. One Englishman

claimed, "[t]he *French*, indeed, have a great number of such

people called *Couriers de Bois*, as expert in the *Indian* way of

fighting as the *Indians* themselves."[38] Such men could adroitly

join Indian raiding parties, and provide accurate knowledge of

many of the waters and lands armies would be obliged to navigate.

Finally, with wilderness skills generally mastered among many

Canadians, France possessed the ability to form the most

formidable and useful troops on the continent. Drilled in the best

skills of both regular and irregular soldiers, the Troupes de la

Marine represented some of the best warriors who marched into

battle in the 1750s. While possessing the discipline of a regular

soldier, they practiced irregular tactics, allowed increased

independence in officers, and did not commission officers on any

factor other than merit. Such troops, combined with the less-

disciplined but still skilled Canadian militia, proved a formidable

group for British generals to match.[39]

The British could depend on "a superior force of Militia to that, which they could raise in Canada."[40] The troops, however, initially proved much less effective than French auxiliaries. Hailing from numerous national origins, and often fiercely independent, British officers soon found that colonial officials and citizens only begrudgingly lent aid to military operations. Even when such aid materialized, colonists typically possessed few armaments and lacked essential martial and wilderness skills. Overall, provincials in the British colonies often proved largely ill-suited for military operations.

Resentful of perceived overbearing authority, provincial in interest, and jealous of neighbors, colonists avoided contributing to military affairs whenever possible. British commanders had a better chance teaching pigs to fly than they did extracting unilateral support from the colonies. Generals pestered governors, and governors wheedled, cajoled and, if all else failed, stormed at provincial assemblies. One enraged governor, Robert Hunter Morris of Pennsylvania, explained, "no Dependance is to be had on the Assembly or people here for any Assistance of

consequence, as they are in such a temper that the danger of their

Country has not the effect upon them that it ought to have."[41]

Even when assemblies authorized military assistance, colonists'

support of deserters sometimes seemed endemic. Recruiters

further realized "the Difficulty of raising of Men" because "they

have neither Courage, Spirits, or Conduct."[42] The frequent

reluctance of colonial assemblies and citizens to contribute to the

war effort sometimes stripped the British of their one

overwhelming advantage: manpower. Local interests and

jealousies further hampered the war effort by denying military

commanders a cohesively united base of operations, source of

supply, and reservoir of potential soldiers.

The cultural landscape of Pennsylvania, as in other

colonies, did not lend itself to unity. Following small initial

settlement by Swedes, Pennsylvania saw an influx of English,

Welsh, and Irish Quakers fleeing persecution in Great Britain.

Although English peoples maintained the largest population into the mid-eighteenth century, the more visible Germans and Scotch-Irish quickly overshadowed them. Religion remained a major motivator, and by 1752 as many as 100,000 Protestant Germans resided in Pennsylvania.[43] One contemporary believed arrivals mounted to "4 to 8000 Palentines [Germans] to Pennsylvania per ann." with more coming as "they encouraged their friends throughout the German empire to come over to them."[44] Sturdy farmers, Germans did not possess the martial skills of their French neighbors to the north, despite their proclivity to absorb immigrating French Huguenots. Rather than breaking new land on the frontier, most Germans preferred moving into previously settled areas on the fringe of the wilderness. Beyond German settlement, often blazing the way, stood the famous Scotch-Irish settlers. With large-scale immigration beginning around 1717, the Scotch-Irish came to dominate the early frontier west of the Susquehanna River. These settlers gained reputations as frontiersmen, although they also struggled against the skill, tenacity, and resourcefulness of their French and Indian foes.[45]

Just as French experiences and activities favored the acquisition of wilderness skills, English experience in the colonies often denied similar development. Heirs to a tradition considering the forest a forbidding place, most colonists settled themselves as farmers, tradesmen, and fishermen. Neither cultivated fields, smoky workshops, nor rolling waves served to foster awareness of the wilderness. In fact, the amateur nature of many British colonists remained so widespread, even towards the end of the eighteenth century, that Moravian missionary John Heckewelder recorded the Indian's low opinion of Anglo-Americans' skills.[46] For example, Heckewelder's Indians noted:

> "the whites are not so attentive as they are [the Indians] to choosing an open dry spot for their encampment; that they will at once set themselves down in any dirty and wet place, provided they are under large trees; that they never look about to see which way the wind blows, so as to be able to lay the wood for their fires in such a position that the smoke may not blow on them; neither do they look up the trees to see whether there are not dead limbs that may fall on them while they are asleep."[47]

The account goes on and on identifying Anglo-American inability to master even the simplest of woodland skills. Even George Washington, ardent supporter of provincial abilities, agreed that provincials posed an uneven match to Indians in the woods. He noted, "I cannot conceive the best white men to be equal to them [Indians] in the Woods."[48] Despite popular belief, therefore, soldiers raised in the British colonies usually possessed no greater aptitude for wilderness warfare than did their red-coated counterparts from across the Atlantic Ocean.[49] To compound this inexperience, provincial soldiers lacked additional attributes useful to their use as auxiliary troops.

Throughout the Seven Year's War, especially at the outset and especially in Pennsylvania, colonies experienced a severe shortage of firearms. One contemporary declared, "[i]n some Colonies there is no Appearance at all of a Militia; and in some others there may be an Appearance of such, but none of Service; whatever there are being poorly armed."[50] While the lack of arms further demonstrates the inexperience of provincials to modern observers, the absence of weapons presented concrete problems for wartime leaders. In 1755, Pennsylvania road builders hacking their way westward across the colony required detachments of General Braddock's army to protect them. Later, when British forces had been moved to other sectors of the North American theater, and Pennsylvania remained alone to fend for itself, this critical shortage of firearms became crucial.[51] Finally, besides the low levels of experience and weaponry, colonial soldiers often possessed one additional incapacitating trait.

British colonists tended to display querulous and unruly natures. To the disciplined British regular, this individualistic trait often proved endlessly frustrating. Braddock, on his 1755 campaign to attack Fort Duquesne, raged, "it has cost infinite pains and labour to bring them [provincials] to any sort of Regularity and Discipline: Their Officers very little better, and all complaining of the ill Usage of the Country."[52] Other British commanders and contemporaries came to the same conclusion.[53]

Although colonists tended to be inexperienced, unarmed, and undisciplined, some understood how to remedy the former.

If provincials wished to gain knowledge and skill in the forest, they need look no further than their North American neighbor across the porous frontier line. Literally bred to be woodland warriors, Indian men represented potential tutors for colonists.[54] Some provincials came to understand that "young men being encouraged to go among the *Indians*, [was] the only way of breeding rangers."[55] Others had to learn the hard way "by observing their manoeuvres when in action against us."[56] The Seven Years' War and Revolutionary War veteran James Smith noted the results of such an education, whether in a positive or negative context, arguing that "[h]ad the British King attempted to enslave us before Braddock's war, in all probability he might readily have done it, because...we were unacquainted with any kind of war."[57] Indeed, for those willing to open their eyes and let go their European pretensions, skillful teachers resided in the woods just beyond the cultivated farmlands of colonial settlement.

The frequent French allies and potential English tutors entered the Seven Years' War, in many ways, during a period of change. Politics, economics, and warfare had all been altered from traditional norms. In some ways, these changes hampered Indians in their struggle to gain a position of power between the two warring empires of France and Great Britain. In other ways, changes lent aid.

At one time, prior to European contact, natives of North America lived in great population centers that sometimes approached comparison with the great nations of Mesoamerica. For various reasons, possibly including a reduction in agricultural output caused by the "Little Ice Age", large centers of population had fragmented into much smaller, kin-based clans typically of five hundred to two thousand. Although these groups might be linked by very loose confederacies, they remained largely autonomous and possessed no central authority from which to unite. This initial lack of unity proved a difficulty in efforts to resist European encroachments. By 1750, however, population levels had dropped an estimated ninety percent east of the

Mississippi through epidemic diseases and colonial encroachment.

This reduction may actually have aided in the process of joining

together scattered bands back into larger population centers now

known as the historic tribes. Thus, by the mid-eighteenth century,

often due to stresses brought about by European contact, Native

peoples had gone full-circle and begun to centralize to a limited

degree.[58]

Native economies had long been dependent on combining

agricultural and wild resources. With the arrival of the Europeans,

however, Indians entered the world economic system, most

notably in the fur trade. While this transformation often led to

dependence, it also offered initial benefits in the form of material

conveniences. Many warriors found that the cost of trading for

guns and providing for their upkeep took less time than

manufacturing their own projectile weapons. Furthermore,

weapons such as the shotgun allowed the bagging of smaller game

heretofore too difficult to hunt for any but the most skilled bowmen. To the Indian male, the economic changes directly translated into increasingly available time for hunting and warfare.[59] And the mid-eighteenth century provided plenty of opportunities for war.

War had always been important to Indian cultures, but it had also been limited. Without the material resources for prolonged war, natives had typically fought vengeance wars, designed more for prisoners, experience, and honor than territory and military gain. Warriors knew their traditional enemies, and thus paid little attention to new tactics, weapons, or increased size of enemy forces. Enemies often considered each other animals rather than full humans, which legitimized the taking of lives. When death occurred, many tribes carried off the lifeless bodies. To defend against attackers, pre-contact villages often possessed wooden palisades. When battle began, Natives formed ranks similar to ancient battles the world over and fought with clubs and bows and countered with wooden armor and shields. The guerilla tactics used so widely in the Seven Years' War likely developed in response to the firepower of European armaments.[60]

The new tactics being developed by Indians after European contact had abundant time to be refined. Agriculture remained predominantly a female task, and young Indian boys trained rigorously in the ways of hunting, warfare, and weaponry.[61] "I...consider this practice of putting boys under perturbation," argued Heckewelder, "as a kind of military school or exercise, intended to create in them a more than ordinary courage, and make them undaunted warriors."[62] The boys learned self-control early, so as not to alert game or enemies. They cut and burned themselves to see how long the pain could be endured. They bathed in cold water daily to inure themselves of hardship. Even games engineered strength, skill, and resourcefulness. Other rituals taught them how to go long periods without food or water, and boys also trained in long-distance running. Training resulted in a physical endurance unmatched by any but the sturdiest of Europeans. Technical skills, such as marksmanship, completed the training.[63] Formerly a prisoner, an impressed James Smith reported, "[a]s they are a sharp, active kind of people, and war is their principle study, in this they have arrived at considerable perfection."[64] A major part of a young boy's training, near infallible woodland skills allowed Indians to employ their finely tuned irregular tactics.

To Native Americans, hunting and warfare did not entirely separate themselves from one another. As one Englishman noted, "[t]he native Inhabitants, the Indians, of this Country, are all Hunters, all the Laws of Nations they know are the Laws of Sporting."[65] Indeed, the way with which Indians went about war seemed like a hunt. Heckewelder noticed the similarities. Like calling in a turkey, scattered war parties could easily find each other through the use of bird and other animal calls. The same calls could be effectively used to draw unsuspecting enemy hunters into ambush. And like tracking a deer during a fall hunt, Native warriors could determine friend from foe merely from a footprint in the earth. To avoid such measures being used against them, warriors walked on hard surfaces whenever possible, and where not possible they might spread themselves widely to avoid ambush or walk in each other's footsteps to conceal their numbers.[66] In addition to their ability to move largely undetected in the woods, Indians did not require the transportation of food because "they can find their subsistence in travelling from their gun."[67] These techniques and more allowed warriors to function well in the wilderness, and the tactics that complimented their forest skills made them formidable opponents.

Indian tactics involved intricate deception, concealment, and timing. Although they sometimes attempted to burn or burrow their way into fortifications, actual assaults rarely occurred.[68] Most often, according to one European contemporary, "their way of making war is by sudden attacks upon exposed places."[69] Exposure of an enemy could be created through a favorite tactic: ambush. To achieve surprise, Native Americans became adept at cover and deception. Trees and bushes concealed attacking warriors, masterful woodland skills allowed undetected movements, and exaggerated numbers often terrified opponents into panic. Due to training in the hunt, aimed fire proved devastating to enemy soldiers. To get in position, war parties executed delicate maneuvers during the heat of battle. When conditions proceeded favorably, circles and half-moons could be formed to damage an enemy on all possible fronts, and if conditions turned against them, hollow squares could be formed for effective defense. Moreover, the light equipage carried by typical warriors allowed them to perform such maneuvers extremely quickly. At all times, combat tactics revolved around the preservation of one's own force. Unlike Europeans, victory alone did not justify high casualty rates. Indians did not feel disgrace at retreating to await more favorable opportunities. Therefore, what European allies sometimes considered cowardice in reality represented a strict adherence to Indian values. Native warriors simply did not stay put and slug it out with an enemy.[70] It did not, however, mean that Indian warriors lacked discipline.

European officers commonly considered natives uncivilized rabble. The ability of such peoples to be disciplined remained out of the question in their minds. General Forbes referred to "their natural fickle disposition."[71] Major Robert Rogers believed they had "no stated rules of discipline."[72] Both men achieved successes, and yet, reality escaped both officers. James Smith possessed a clearer view of the true nature of Indian warriors. As if responding to such officers as Forbes and Rogers, Smith argued, "I have often heard the British officers call the Indians the undisciplined savages, which is a capital mistake–as they have all the essentials of discipline." He went on to say, "they are under good command, and punctual in obeying orders: they can act in concert, and when their officers lay a plan and give orders, they will chearfully unite in putting all their directions into immediate execution."[73] While such a broad stroke can hardly be applied to all Indians, Smith's contemporary Heckewelder reported very similar traits. Interestingly, he too stressed punctuality as an essential attribute of Indians in warfare.[74]

Therefore, despite much popular opinion amongst Europeans, Native Americans did indeed possess adequate amounts of discipline. Such discipline based itself upon individual honor and strong leadership.

Whereas discipline in European armies might be enforced through fear of severe punishment, Native Americans depended upon individual honor. Indian warriors did not worry about physical punishments. They faced the much harsher threat of societal shame. Such chastisements typically answered the purpose of creating discipline. War leaders tended to be highly respected members of Indian society, and as such, warriors fought fiercely to gain their recognition. Meritorious behavior gained followers and garnered prestige. In the long run, accomplishments led to status, unlike hereditary European societies.[75] Thus, leadership in war bands tended to be both strong and respected, and therefore extremely effective.

Although both the French and the British ultimately recruited irregular warriors from among their own citizens and through alliances with Indian groups, varying strategies and goals dictated different levels of importance to be placed upon such soldiers. The French did conduct offensive operations against British strongholds, but the possession of desired areas and tremendous internal lines of supply and communication naturally led them into a defensive stance. Skilled Canadian irregulars and large numbers of Indian allies proved crucial to the defense of frontier posts.

For a variety of reasons, the French government did not commit large numbers of regular troops to the North American conflict. British command of the ocean, and the resultant risk and expense of getting regulars to Canada, combined with French concerns on the European continent perhaps led to such low numbers of regular forces in North America. Perhaps also the French realized what one British planner did, that "[t]he French, being already possess'd of the Lakes & Rivers at the Back of the English Settlements from Quebeck to the Missisippi, can easily bring their whole Force to...any one Point."[76] In control of defensive positions of their choosing and blessed with incredible internal lines of transportation the French could survive with relatively few regulars. To fill the gap and offset British numbers, French leaders relied heavily upon the skill of Canadian and Indian irregulars. [77]

French dependence upon its irregulars depended upon several premises. First, the French understood that while they possessed short supply lines, the British would be forced to travel great distances from their centers of power. Armies operating out of such areas could be kept off balance by irregular raiding. Raids could thus bleed and bog down British advances before they gained an opportunity to pierce the periphery of French defenses.[78] The hope remained that "the English shoud be tired with the fruitless expense."[79] While military assaults could be dealt with in such a way, the war could be brought to the English doorsteps through raids by small groups of combined native and Canadian warriors. Not unlike modern terrorism, the goal would be to make colonists sicken of war with France.[80] While these techniques possessed obvious advantages, they also posed difficulties in the long run.

Small raids and delaying actions worked well against disorganized and undisciplined enemies. But as Britain's forces slowly grew and organized, such tactics increasingly became less effective. Morris astutely noted, "unless the Enemy can get some advantage of that kind [surprise] they stand no chance."[81] Indeed, although British irregulars could rarely match their French and Indian counterparts in guerilla skills, the tide of numbers as well as British strategies increasingly made such skills less relevant.[82]

In forest warfare, British regulars and irregulars fought at a disadvantage against their experienced French and Indian foes. Equipment often weighed too much to make essential quick movements, bayonets could not be used to maximum effectiveness in the broken terrain, and the very closeness of the troops that allowed the bayonets' effectiveness made the same soldiers vulnerable targets to well-concealed opponents. Experienced frontier leaders such as John Armstrong and Bouquet acknowledged this.[83] The advantages such troops presented

towards the ultimate goals of British leaders, however, offset these

disadvantages.

British strategy ultimately centered upon capturing the

major French strongholds, not upon harassment of French supply

lines and civilians. Ideally suited for such operations, British

forces targeted the weakness of the French position.[84] One

military planner pinpointed it, arguing that if the "[l]ink of the

Chain betwixt Canada and the Ohio being once broke would

probably make the French abandon their present Undertaking."[85]

The French did possess relatively reliable internal transportation

routes. If vital locations on those routes could be captured,

however, the whole system broke down. Therefore, the distant

posts fell by default with the capture of posts closer to French

centers of power and supply.[86] Small group raiding, as conducted

by the French, could not successfully combat British aims

permanently.

To accomplish its goals, Britain could only depend upon highly disciplined troops to assault and maintain a siege around an enemy fortification. Such men could be depended upon to stand their ground and absorb casualties in the cause of victory, to mass their numbers, to deliver devastating volley fire and bayonet charges, to secure and hold advantageous positions, and most importantly, to follow orders unquestionably. For these reasons and more, rigid discipline allowed Europeans to make ordinary citizens into formidable warriors without the lifelong training provided in native cultures.[87] One soldier commended his commanding officer, George Washington, because, "[y]ou took us under your tuition...trained us up in the practice of that discipline which alone can constitute good troops."[88] Therefore, if British strategy depended so heavily upon its regular, disciplined troops, irregulars played a decidedly secondary role.

Since fortifications became the primary target of British military operations, the forests became less important. Instead of a place to be conquered, they simply represented a place to pass through, though admittedly with difficulty. The British

understood that "[i]n an American Campaign...victories are not

decisive, but defeats are ruinous."[89] The role of the irregulars was

thus to prevent ruinous defeats. They proved most effective

teamed with regulars, to serve on the flanks and rear, preventing

surprise. If contact occurred, they could provide covering fire and

perform flanking maneuvers. In effect, British irregular operations

in the Ohio country, while aiding in ultimate victory, occurred

along the peripheries while regulars executed campaigns that

brought conflicts to a close.[90]

CHAPTER 2

"A Charming Field for an Encounter"

After Major George Washington's polite rebuke at the hands of the French during the winter of 1753-1754, Governor Robert Dinwiddie of Virginia determined to beat the French at their own game. He scraped together a small number of Virginian troops and appealed for aid from the neighboring colonies. The governor then dispatched his puny force to build a fortification at the forks of the Ohio, where the Allegheny and Monongahela Rivers meet to form the Ohio River. Dinwiddie once again turned to Washington to perform an important task. While a small advanced party under Captain William Trent began construction of the fort, and the overall commander Colonel Joshua Fry tarried in the rear, Washington set out on April 2nd with approximately 165 soldiers including a Swedish volunteer to "endeavour to make the road sufficiently good for the heaviest artillery to pass, and...fortify ourselves as strongly the short time will allow."[1]

When Ensign Edward Ward, then in command of the operations at the Forks, surrendered the works on April 18th, to a far superior French force, Washington's command abruptly became the advance of the army. The situation quickly escalated as Washington and his opposite, Captain Claude Pierre Pecaudy, seigneur de Contrecoeur, suddenly found themselves in close proximity and unsure of the other's intentions. Both began dispatching small scouting parties to ascertain the location, strength, and possible plans of the enemy.[2]

Convinced that "the French must pass our Camp, which I flatter myself is not practicable with't my having intelligence," Washington launched several parties. They included groups of loyal Indians and one, on May 10th, under the command of Adam Stephen. Nearly simultaneously, Contrecoeur directed Ensign Joseph Coulon de Villiers de Jumonville to undertake a similar mission. In the vastness of the woods, the two parties missed each other, but on reports of Jumonville's presence Washington sent a second, stronger party of 130 men to locate the French ensign.

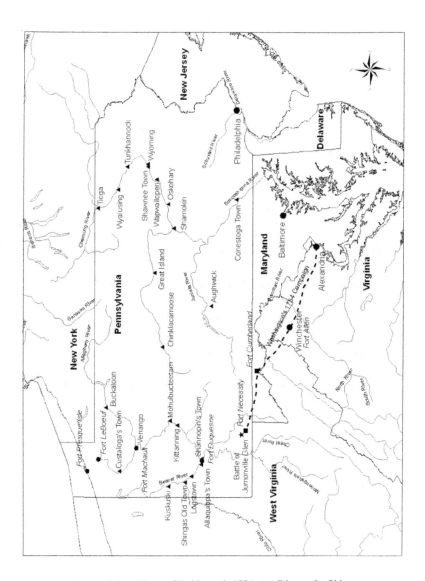

Map 1: Colonel George Washington's 1754 expedition to the Ohio.

When they too failed to meet the French scouts, and with the arrival of more concrete information about their location, Washington rounded up many of his remaining men and marched off towards a fateful encounter.[3]

On the evening of May 27th, around eleven o'clock at night, Washington departed in search of the French encampment. He took with him forty Virginians and anywhere from five to twelve Indian allies, among them the Ohio Iroquoian leader Tanacharison.[4] The rain fell so heavily, and the men found the night so dark, that "we lost seven Men on the March, and were five Hours in marching as many Miles."[5] At sunrise, two men scouted the French position while the remainder tried their best to put their sodden arms and ammunition in good order. When the scouts returned, Washington and his Indian counterpart agreed to surround the French encampment.[6]

In a secluded depression, thirty-seven French soldiers went about their morning activities. Some cooked breakfast while others lingered near the bark huts they had slept in. British accounts agree that when the French detected their attackers, they quickly snatched up their arms and prepared for battle. Most accounts also indicate that the French fired first. Regardless, it remains certain that hot fire erupted between both sides. Sheltered in the bark huts, French firearms functioned well. One Englishman died and three more received wounds. Washington's men also delivered fire, but finding some of the ammunition damp they pressed close with fixed bayonets. After about ten or fifteen minutes, the French broke and ran in the opposite direction. Finding retreat cut off by the Indians, who had circled around during the melee, the routed soldiers fled back to the English victors to surrender their arms. Washington reported killing ten French, wounding one, and capturing twenty-one prisoners. At least one Frenchmen escaped to deliver the news to Contrecoeur at the Forks of the Ohio. Flushed with victory even while knowing the superior French would be informed of the encounter, Washington returned to his encampment with his prisoners. Shortly afterwards, on June 6th, his old companion Christopher

Gist arrived informing the colonel that Colonel Fry had died in a riding accident. The burden of command thus fell on Washington until Fry's replacement, Colonel Innes, could arrive.[7] Before that happened, however, events reached their climax.

While ill-advisedly deciding to continue his drive towards the Forks of the Ohio, Washington learned that a much larger force of French soldiers and Indian warriors was on the move. He fell back to the Great Meadows and began construction of the appropriately named Fort Necessity, which consisted of nothing more than shallow trenches and a flimsy, circular palisade. Now joined by a South Carolina independent company of regulars, Washington's army consisted of about four hundred men.[8] "Nothing but very unequal numbers," Washington reported to Dinwiddie, "shall engage me to submit or Retreat."[9] Unequal numbers arrived on July 3rd when approximately seven hundred French and Indians placed the English force under attack.

Washington presented his troops in regular formation in a field outside his hastily built fortifications. The French declined such an encounter, and instead chose to take cover in the surrounding woods. This movement sent the English scurrying back to the trenches and palisade. Hot fire erupted between both sides until evening, when a sudden downpour reduced many British soldiers to arming themselves with only bayonet-fixed muskets. During the night of July 3rd, apparently not perceiving the dire plight of the sodden British soldiers inside Fort Necessity, the French commander offered relatively generous terms to Washington for his surrender. Thus, on July 4th, Washington's army marched south. The battle ended with thirty dead and seventy wounded on the British side. The French, despite attacking a fortified position, lost far less. With Washington's surrender, and the resultant end of the British campaign, the French commanded undisputed possession of the Ohio country.[10]

Washington's defeat at Fort Necessity did not result from French irregular tactics and Washington's lack of irregulars to counter them. Nor did it result from overwhelming French numbers. Instead, defeat stemmed from Washington's lack of firepower and adequate supplies, his men's low level of discipline and experience, and finally his failure to formulate sound decisions.

Partly due to fear of the large French army, and partly because Washington "took upon him to Command the Indians as his slaves" and "would never listen to them," Iroquoian Indians under the leadership of Tanaghrisson had indeed abandoned him at the critical hour.[11] Under such treatment, such an outcome does not seem unexpected. By the time of the battle, perhaps six or seven Indians remained in the camp.[12] As a result, Washington lacked the Indian irregulars that the French possessed. Yet, Washington held a fortification, and irregular troops traditionally did not experience success in assaults. Therefore, Washington's position should have protected him from such troops, and nullified his own lack of irregulars.

Washington also faced a numerically superior enemy. Although the young Virginian placed French attackers at 1,500, and another witness believed them to amount to nine hundred, in reality they probably consisted of seven hundred combined French and Indian warriors. Washington possessed about four hundred men.[13] Once again, due to the fortification, his numbers should have allowed him to hold the position against a force less than double his size. Despite these favorable conditions, other factors conspired to compel the colonel's surrender.

On one level, Washington's men lacked the essential firepower to repel the French aggressions and supplies to carry on operations. Washington had hoped that Dinwiddie would "see the absolute necessity for our having...a number of cannon, some of heavy metal, with mortars and grenadoes to attack the French, and put us on an equal footing with them."[14] Yet, despite the British government's gift of thirty artillery pieces to Virginia, only ten of them had reached Alexandria by the time of the fighting. Washington only had nine swivel guns with which to defend the fort when the French arrived.[15]

Even the men's small arms proved ineffectual in the defense of the fort. Due to the late afternoon's rainfall, virtually all of the ammunition became damp. Soldiers frantically

attempted drying their weapons. But only two screws, tools used

to clear the useless ammunition out of wet muskets, had been

brought on the expedition.[16] With limited access to the screws,

Washington found his command "left...with nothing but a few (for

all were not provided with them) bayonets for defense."[17] Thus

Washington's firepower left him in no position to defeat the

French outright, and his men's condition left them in no position

to outlast a siege.

At the beginning of the expedition, Washington found his

men woefully underdressed. "There is Scarce a Coat, or Waistcoat

to their Backs;" he announced, "In short, they are as illy provided

as can well be conceiv'd."[18] Washington feared "the great

necessity for Cloathing the Men...renders them very incapable of

the necessary Service, as they must unavoidably be expos'd to

inclement weather."[19] By the evening of July 3rd, as the men lay

exposed to the very inclement weather Washington feared, their

clothes had been reduced to tatters. The colonel provided new clothing almost immediately after his army's return to Virginia.[20] And yet, even with sufficient firepower and clothing, Washington's men would have been no match for the French in the undisciplined state he found them.

At the beginning of the campaign, Washington reported discouragement in respect to his soldiers. With many officers yet to arrive, he experienced "a fatiguing time to me, in managing a number of selfwilled, ungovernable people."[21] Conditions only worsened during the campaign. The refusal of the South Carolinian independent regulars to do any manual labor "had an unhappy Effect on our Men; for they no sooner learnt that it was not the proper duty of Soldiers to perform these Services, than they became as backward as the Independents."[22] Then, when Captain Trent's troops arrived after their expulsion at the forks, Washington reluctantly ordered them away. He had found "their refractory Behavior" to be "rather injurious to the other Men."[23] The men's natural disposition combined with the negative examples set by the South Carolinian independent regulars and

Trent's soldiers finally snapped what semblance of discipline
Washington had been able to establish on the night of the attack.
According to the accounts of both Adam Stephen and Dan Claus,
more than half of Washington's men stormed the supply stockade
during the night of July 3rd and proceeded to intoxicate
themselves. Their combat effectiveness, already eroded by other
factors, suddenly diminished even more. Finally, Washington
conceded defeat and his rag-tag army withdrew from the Great
Meadows. According to French reports, although in contrast to
Washington's fervent denials, the British forces heaped a final,
inglorious scene on the already embarrassing defeat. Instead of
retreating in a controlled fashion, many succumbed to great
disorder.[24] Despite the blame that can be placed upon
Washington's supplies and men, defeat ultimately resulted from a
string of crucial mistakes made by the commander himself.

Most obviously, Washington had been specifically
instructed to avoid engagements until the entire British force could
be united in one location. Perhaps in self-defense, Governor

Dinwiddie declared after the defeat, "my Orders to the
Commanding Officer was by no means to attack the Enemy till all
the Forces were joined in a Body."[25] Reinforcements were on the
way, and Dinwiddie suggests that Washington understood this.
Even as he fought his losing campaign in western Pennsylvania,
two independent companies from New York and several
companies from the North Carolina Regiment moved in the
direction of the conflict. Washington, however, had acted too
hastily. By refusing to withdraw his troops to a safe location, he
committed his men to combat before they reached maximum
strength.[26] As a result, the unequal odds faced by his army at Fort
Necessity, while not necessarily a deciding factor, should have
been unnecessary.

Also, Washington's defensive measures put the English in
no better position to resist the French. Instead of falling back, he
decided to force a stand at the Great Meadows. In Fort Necessity,
the British frantically prepared a defense against the oncoming
French army. Unfortunately, the fortification remained essentially

useless. By the time the French arrived, it had not even been completed. Furthermore, the walls had been constructed out of split logs instead of full logs, and the hastily built palisade required smaller logs to act as fillers in the gaps between the main logs. Even with the stockade, many of the troops had been required to man posts in shallow trenches dug outside the wall, exposing them to enemy fire from the surrounding woods. Several points of woods allowed effective fire into Washington's position from as close as sixty yards away.[27]

Despite Washington's meager defensive works, had he had his way the battle would have been waged on the open meadow he described as "a charming field for an Encounter."[28] Indeed, when the French arrived, Washington drew his men into formation in the field. When the enemy refused to accept such battle, and fanned out into the adjoining fields, Washington ordered his men back to their woefully prepared defensive positions. Only at that point did Washington and his men fully comprehend the tenuousness of their position, as lead balls rained down upon them in their open trenches and through the gaps in

their split log palisade. The French, for their part, maintained

covered positions in the woods within easy musket range of the

English fortification.[29]

The presence of French irregulars, and the corresponding

absence of such troops on the British side, certainly aided France

during its victory in the Ohio country in 1754. But their abilities

alone did not dictate success for the French. Instead, the British

failure to field an effective regular force must be seen as a leading

cause of their defeat. Washington's failure to await

reinforcements led to numerical inferiority. Britain's failure to

provide adequate firepower in the form of artillery robbed

Washington of a crucial defensive weapon in the battle at the

Great Meadows. The heavy rain further diminished his soldiers'

ability to beat back the French irregulars. The lack of discipline

among the English forces also eroded their abilities as a regular

force. Finally, the lackluster construction of defensive works

denied Washington's men of the one foolproof against irregular

foes: solid, unassailable walls. Thus, when considering all of the
factors leading to Washington's defeat, it cannot simply be
attributed to superior irregular tactics over inferior regular tactics.
Instead, Washington appeared hampered by British logistical
mistakes, the quality of his own men, and his own decision-
making skills.

CHAPTER 3

"Men Dropped like Leaves in Autumn"

After Colonel George Washington's defeat in 1754, and before war had officially been declared between the two empires, British leaders sought a way to remedy their expulsion from the Ohio country. Ultimately, they chose to send General Edward Braddock with the 44th and 48th Regiments of British regular soldiers. For one of the first times in European North America, Great Britain committed a large force of regular troops to its colonies. When Braddock arrived in February 1755, many provincials assumed their problems had been solved. Surely this professional officer with a strong, well-trained army would clear the upstart French from the contested lands in western Pennsylvania. Virginia and North Carolina raised troops to aid in the effort.[1] Although they provided no troops, Philadelphians giddily gathered fireworks in preparation for a victory celebration. Not influenced by the exuberance of his peers, Benjamin Franklin cautioned, "[t]he events of war are subject to great uncertainty."[2]

Indeed, what happened next went beyond most Briton's wildest nightmares.

Braddock, his British and provincial troops, artillery train, and heavy baggage set out towards the French positions at Fort Duquesne closely following Washington's route from a year earlier. Now an aid to the general, Washington passed the scene of his previous defeat. This time Washington belonged to a much larger and presumably more powerful force. The army, however, moved much too slowly for Braddock. Splitting his forces, he left part with the baggage to slowly follow and led the remaining 1,300 at a quicker pace towards their destination at the forks of the Ohio. They moved relatively unopposed, until July 9th when they crossed the Monongahela River for the final time.[3]

With an advanced party several hundred yards beyond the main body of the army, the British proceeded to move on Fort Duquesne at the point where the Allegheny and Monongahela Rivers meet. The party, however, slammed into a group of 891 French, Canadians, and Indians. Firing broke out between the two

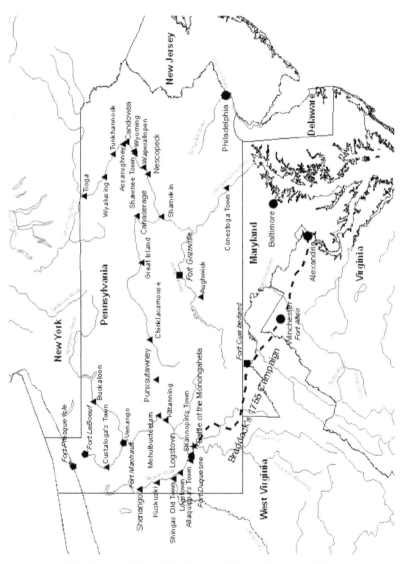

Map 2: General Edward Braddock's 1755 expedition to the Ohio.

sides and the French commander fell dead. Despite the loss of their leader, the Canadians and Indians quickly fanned out along the British advance party's flanks and placed it under a deadly fire. Hearing the eruption of conflict, Braddock elected to send a relief party to aid his advance. The timing could not have been worse. As the fresh force rushed forward, the beleaguered advance party broke and fled for the rear. The troops ran into one another, mingling the wounded, terrified, and confused with the previously intact relief unit. The integrity of both units quickly disappeared, and a rout ultimately commenced.[4]

Despite the reigning confusion and hail of roundballs, British forces managed to maintain a defense for over two hours. As more and more officers fell wounded and dead, and with the fatal wounding of Braddock, panic eventually ensued and a pell-mell retreat began. At the cost of twenty-three dead and sixteen wounded, the French and Indians not only repelled the British advance, but also annihilated two thirds of the attacking force. The victory had an additional, unexpected effect, as the shattered

British army retreated to the slower moving party Braddock had previously left behind. Panic erupted anew and the British army ultimately abandoned the expedition and withdrew to Philadelphia.[5]

When news of the defeat became known to the public, some angrily denounced the British officers' failure to heed advice regarding the peculiar skills and fighting styles of the French irregular forces. Governor Morris of Pennsylvania quickly blamed Braddock and his officers. Writing William Shirley, who succeeded as the Commander in Chief in North America after Braddock's death, Morris ranted on July 30th, "our Defeat was owing to the want of Conduct in the Commanders, who suffered themselves to fall into an Ambuscade" that "made the slaughter more terrible." The slaughter resulted from "the General and his Officers persisting in the Men's keeping their Ranks and firing in platoons."[6] A survivor, Adam Stephen, agreed with Morris. He argued that "his Excellency found to his woeful Experience, what had frequently been told him, that formal attacks & Platoon firing never would answer against the Savages and Candeans."[7] Yet, despite the blame that ultimately fell on the defenseless general, he had made arrangements to prepare for the type of battle he entered. Even though Braddock did resort to regular tactics against his irregular adversary, his well-disciplined and well-trained force could have emerged victorious.

Arriving in North America with two regiments of British regular troops, Braddock brought with him the trappings of a heavily supplied European force. His critic, Adam Stephen, argued, "you might as well send a Cow in pursuit of a Hare as an English soldier loaded…with a Coat, Jacket, &c. &c. &c. after Canadeans in their Shirts, who can shoot and run well, or Naked Indians accustomed to the woods."[8] Although Braddock did not possess a wealth of actual combat experience, many of his officers and men had undergone warfare in the rough country of Scotland against irregular typed warriors. As a result, whether the idea belonged to Braddock or his trusted subordinates, steps had been taken to more adequately prepare the regulars for wilderness warfare.[9] As a result, Braddock "lighten'd them [regulars] as much as possible, and have left in store their Swords and the greatest part of their heavy Accoutrements."[10] Such measures assured that the British regulars, and the already more lightly accoutered Virginians and North Carolinians, possessed less burdensome loads than most European armies at the time. Finally, as the campaign inched along, Braddock showed flexibility as he chose to leave his heavy baggage trailing behind and forged ahead with a quicker moving force. Thus, although Braddock's army did indeed possess heavier equipment than an irregular force, he had made strides towards streamlining his troops.[11]

Although Braddock depended upon his regulars for a successful completion to his campaign, he still needed irregulars to shepherd his force through the wilderness, provide intelligence, and alert him to any surprises. Prior to his expedition, the general had been repeatedly lectured by colonial do-gooders about the necessity of such troops. After his defeat, many also indicted Braddock for his failure to raise irregular troops for the expedition.[12] "There were but few of them [irregulars] engaged,"

Adam Stephen argued, "as General Braddock had unhappily

placed his confidence and whole Dependence on the Regiments."[13]

Much of this perception, however, appears to be the result of

Braddock's hostile and haughty exterior rather than his actual

actions. He often appeared disrespectful towards the provincials

and Indians willing to help him.[14] "The savages may indeed be a

formidable enemy to your raw American militia," Braddock said

to Benjamin Franklin in his famous line, "but upon the King's

regulars and disciplined troops, Sir, it is impossible they should

make any impression."[15] Instead of arrogance, this might be seen

as an act of bravado meant to bolster the confidence of his army.

In fact, the general worried in private about his lack of irregulars.[16]

Writing to England, Braddock lamented, "you conceive the

difficulty of getting good Intelligence, all I have is from

Indians."[17] Thus, if the general was at fault for failing to recruit

sufficient irregular troops to compliment his regulars, it appears more the result of a personality flaw than the lack of intelligence,

desire, or military acumen.

Despite Braddock's reported arrogance, Indians did join

his expedition to serve as scouts. Scaroudy, the Iroquoian

chieftain in the Ohio country, actively recruited Indians to the

campaign and ultimately sacrificed his son for his efforts. George

Croghan, the experienced Pennsylvanian trader, also delivered

native warriors to Braddock's campaign. As late as July, a soldier

named Jacob Huber reported officers arriving in camp with allied

Indians.[18] Although the numbers remained small, the combined

Anglo-Indian scouts' numbers reached high enough levels by June

28th to "scour the Country."[19]

While the British scrambled to gather small but effective

scouting parties, the French possessed them in abundance.

Contrecoeur, the commander at Fort Duquesne, did not hesitate to

deploy them against the advancing army. Small, irregular parties

proceeded to harass the British force. The British, for their part,

perceived the attacks as merely an annoyance meant only to retard their movements. Few believed the raiding parties posed any real

threat to the regular army of General Braddock.[20] In fact, the

parties proved so unsuccessful that Contrecoeur conceded, "I have

not ceased…to send out detachments of French and Indians to

harry the English…These troops kept on their guard so well,

marching always in battle order that all efforts which the

detachments made against them were useless."[21] The British were

thus in a relatively strong and confident position, and the French

remained skeptical of their abilities, when 891 French, Canadian,

and Indian irregular and regular troops set out to attack the British

as they made their final crossing of the Monongahela River.[22]

    In such a situation, the French and British waged battle on

July 9, 1755. The French force heavily contained Canadian and

Indian irregular warriors. The British army alternatively

predominated in traditional, regular troops. The battle, however,

cannot simply be seen as a victory of irregular over regular tactics.

Instead, both sides possessed unique advantages and

disadvantages. Battlefield conditions, the decisions that affected

them, and the quality of troops involved ultimately decided the
outcome.

The terrain through which the British marched certainly
favored the French, Canadian, and Indian ambushers. As
Braddock's army crossed the Monongahela River for the last time
and moved towards Fort Duquesne, the carpenters cut a road
flanked by hills. Many English survivor accounts stress the
importance of the hills on the outcome of the battle.[23] One English
officer named Cameron noted, "[t]he Enemy were advantageously
posted on two Hills, one on each Side of our Way, which Hills
joined in our Front."[24] Another more directly indicated the
importance of the prominences, saying, "[w]e found that we
should never gain ye day unless we dislodged them from the rising
ground."[25]

In fact, the ground proved so advantageous that it comes
as no surprise that the French had previously scouted and decided
upon utilizing the position. Unfortunately for the attackers, the
British advance guard had reached the point of ambush at nearly

the same time. The enemies exchanged fire, and the French commander fell dead in the first volley. At this point, the British missed their first golden opportunity to take control of the battle. As the French and Indians wavered with the loss of their leader, the British did not press their advantage. The attackers quickly regrouped, and the British then missed the second opportunity to establish a dominant position. A lack of decisive action allowed the resurgent French to filter around the flanks of the British and seize the high ground they had originally planned to occupy.[26] The resultant conflict thus proved spontaneous rather than well planned, but quick French action and a sluggish British response provided the attackers with the upper hand.

As the French held the line to the front of the British advance guard, the Canadians and Indians found themselves at home on the wooded slopes above the British position. As they gradually enveloped Braddock's army, the irregulars managed to hide and move about enough to protect themselves from enemy fire.[27] So elusive were the French irregulars that one Englishman later noted, "If we saw of them five or six at one time [it] was a great sight."[28] In fact, survivor accounts cite enemy numbers anywhere from Washington's low estimate of three hundred to a certain Cameron's inflated belief that the British had been outnumbered. Other accounts fall variously in between, proving the skill with which the Canadians and Indians managed to conceal themselves.[29]

The very qualities that made the French irregulars effective snipers, however, kept the attacking force perilously close to defeat. They had already almost fled during the initial contact with the British advance guard. Then, English artillery began spewing grapeshot into the surrounding woods. While not particularly effective in a physical sense, the psychological impact on the irregulars had immediate results. According to French accounts, Canadian and Indian warriors began retreating under the strain of the artillery barrage. According to the French, only the image of the regulars, steadfastly holding the line in front of the British position, encouraged the irregulars to maintain the attack.[30]

Finally, the sniping action of the Canadians and Indians did not possess the power to deliver a decisive blow to the defending troops below. British inaction, confusion, and poor decision-making aided the irregulars in their efforts. One French participant put it best, noting, "[t]he battle was unyielding on both sides, and success was long in doubt, but at last the enemy collapsed."[31]

Entering the battle, however, the British possessed several key advantages over the French as well. Many contemporaries, among them Adam Stephen and Governor Morris, condemned Braddock's failure to adequately cover his advancing army. Morris raged, "our forces were surprized and fell into an Ambuscade for want of the precaution necessary in marching thro' and uninhabited Wilderness."[32] Stephen and other surviving soldiers heaped similar condemnation upon the deceased general. An objective analysis, however, dispels much of the vilification of General Braddock. An advance party had been posted approximately a quarter mile ahead of the main body of the army.

Moreover, the party served its primary function—they drew the fire of the enemy party before the main body could be ambushed, and thus alerted the nearly one thousand men in the rear of danger. In this view, Braddock had avoided what many previously feared—the complete surprise and annihilation of his exposed force. With the warning provided by his beleaguered advance guard, Braddock found himself in a position to counter and possibly defeat the attacking troops.[33]

When the warning came, Braddock should have been able to utilize his regular troops. Much has been made about the wilderness nature of the fighting. Certainly, the advantage the hills provided the French, Canadians, and Indians proved helpful. However, most accounts of the conflict stress the openness of the woods at the point of attack.[34] An Englishman with the advance guard, W. Dunbar, reported, "[t]he Ground from thence to the French Fort, we were told was pretty good, & the woods open."[35] A Frenchman named Roucher confirmed, saying, "our detachment was posted in the woods, it was very clear."[36] Finally, Benjamin

Franklin, who had not been present, concluded from reports that the battle occurred "in a more open part of the woods than any it [the British army] had passed."[37] Under such circumstances, despite the cover vegetation allowed the enemy, the British regulars should have been able to function in their own fashion. Why they did not results primarily not from vegetation but other circumstances.

The final British advantage lay in the main body of the army. Although it reportedly did little physical damage to the attackers, Braddock's artillery had a profound effect, initially, upon the psyche of the Canadian and Indian irregulars. British leaders, however, failed to capitalize upon the early success of their cannon, and ultimately neglected to properly protect the guns from enemy attackers. As a result, the tremendous advantage afforded by the artillery on the British side ended up squandered. Artillery crews had been wiped out before they could readjust fire and increase effectiveness as the battle raged closer to their position.[38]

Despite these initial advantages, poor decision-making and simple bad luck precipitated the reigning confusion that ultimately limited English chances at succeeding. Upon hearing the attack on the advance party, Braddock quickly decided upon rushing a force to the relief of their comrades. Considering the accounts of the open woods, it may have been wise to send troops on either side of the road, thus attacking the French forces in the flanks and at the same time relieving the fire on the advance party's flanks. Instead, getting troops to the point of attack instead of worrying about how they would help when they got there seemed Braddock's primary concern. The general instead chose to rush them directly up the cleared path. Unfortunately, he never had the chance to prove that his stratagem was the wisest. At the same time that troops from the main body rushed towards the attack, the advance party began giving way. The result proved catastrophic to British dispositions and order. The two groups crashed into each other, mingling confused and terrified troops with the intact and orderly relief party. At this point, not only the bloodied and wounded advance guard, but the relief party as well, had lost cohesiveness as a fighting force.[39] "We immediately advanced in order to sustain them [the advance party]," remembered Robert Orme, "but the Detachment of the 200 or 300 gave way and fell back upon us, which caused such confusion and struck so great a panic into our men that afterwards no military Expedient could be made use of that had any effect upon them [the men]."[40] The confusion resulting from the mingling of the two parties significantly exposed the fatal flaw of Braddock's regular army—it could not function, in any environment, without large degrees of order.

Critics often denounced Braddock for his reliance on regular tactics during his ill-fated expedition. Among them, Washington argued against "[t]he folly and consequence of opposing compact bodies to the sparse manner of Indian fighting in woods."[41] On the other end of the battlefield, however, French officers admired the British rank and file marching into battle. The problem did not lay with the massed ranks of Braddock's army, which could have regained control by acting in concert, but instead with the breakdown of those very ranks. Officers on horses became easy marks, and fell beyond their proportion. The men, terrified by the enemy's fire and increasingly leaderless, broke ranks and formed huddled masses on the road.[42] "Such was ye confusion," remembered one survivor, "that ye men were sometimes 20 or 30 deep, & he thought himself securest who was in the center." In such a condition, the men stood no chance to coordinate a united defense, much less a successful counterattack. Often, when soldiers heard someone near them fire, they too fired. In that way, soldiers randomly threw away their rounds at non-existent targets, and volley fire often ceased to occur.[43]

Some officers, primarily consisting of provincials, took it upon themselves to take to the trees and engage the Canadian and Indian irregulars. Although such a decision may have been beneficial had it been ordered and coordinated, the movement served to exacerbate the reigning confusion within the British defenses. Seeing smoke erupting in the woods near them, many soldiers unknowingly fired at their comrades. Many consequently perished from friendly fire while they also drew fire away from the actual attackers. This irregular action thus compromised Braddock's attempt to defend in a regular fashion. It had robbed him of badly needed men, wasted the fire of his British regulars, and deepened the confusion he struggled to deal with. Therefore, British irregulars actually eroded rather than strengthened British attempts to deal with their Canadian and Indian foes.[44] During the resultant confusion, another, preexisting flaw within the British regulars began to emerge.

The men that panicked, bunched up, and fired wildly into the woods did not act as a British regular might be expected to act. Perhaps if they had held their nerve, stayed in formation, and fired on orders, the results may have been different. The fact remains, however, that many of the red-coated soldiers fighting for their lives were not trained British regulars. When the British regiments arrived from England, neither possessed a complete compliment of soldiers. A British report stated, "Sir Peter

Halket's & Colonel Dunbar's Regiments of Foot…consisting of 30. Sergeants, 30. Corporals, 20. Drummers, & 500. private Men, each Regiment; To be augmented to 700., Rank & File, each Regiment in Virginia, No Carolina, So Carolina, Maryland, & Pennsylvania."[45] Raising troops to fill his regiments in those areas, however, Braddock found the men less than satisfactory.[46] Perhaps due to lack of training, some French attributed their victory to the British "not knowing how to fire steadily."[47]

Many of the officers also possessed few, if any, qualifications for donning a red coat. Some had been recalled from half-pay retirement to serve in both the British and provincial regiments.[48] Others had no military training at all, gaining their positions because Washington "had the compliment of several blank Ensigncies given him to dispose of to the Young Gentlemen of his acqe. To supply the vacancies in the 44 and 48 Regts."[49] As a result, many of the officers and the rank and file lacked the training and discipline expected of British regulars.

Some evidence, moreover, indicates that the soldiers went into battle disgruntled. "As to the men," argued one English magazine, "it is said they were extremely dissatisfied with the service to which they were destined from their first coming on shore; that the officers observing this discontent, treated them with a severity that greatly increased it, so that some do not scruple to affirm, that our late loss was nothing more than the effect of a mutiny."[50] Although the statement may simply have been an excuse, survivor accounts almost universally indicate that soldiers refused to heed officers' commands. Washington, Orme, Dunbar, and others bitterly denounced the failure.[51] Intriguingly, two questionable stories arose confirming the extent of the mutinous behavior. One, concerning brothers Joseph and Thomas Fausett, argues that Tom fired the shot that killed Braddock. As the story goes, Joseph took to a tree as the deadly enemy fire began taking its toll. Observing him, Braddock denounced Joseph as a coward and ran him through with a sword. According to Thomas, the fatal shot was both to revenge his brother and to precipitate the retreat

Braddock had previously refused.[52] Another story concerns the

general after his wound. According to one account, Braddock

"was borne from the field by some soldiers whom his aid-de-camp

had bribed to that service by a guinea and a bottle of rum to

each."[53] Here, Braddock's soldiers appear so disgruntled that they

would not even carry their fatally wounded commander from the

field without a bribe. While the stories might be a bit extreme,

their myth developed from a reality—the soldiers of Braddock's

command largely declined to follow the entreaties of their officers.

The ultimate defeat of the British, when viewed from

alternative angles, thus goes beyond mere tactics. It did not occur

simply because French irregulars hid in the woods while English

regulars stood in the open. Rather, defeat resulted from a

conglomerate of situations. "The rout," said one survivor, "is the

fruit of M. Dumas's experience, and of the activity and valor of

those officers under his command."[54] Indeed, the French fought

well and, besides initial faltering by their irregulars, pressed their

advantage. No less valiant, the British fought back well in small groups and as individuals. Their strength, however, lay in coordination. The advance guard had served its function by alerting the main body of the army of danger. Failure to put reinforcements in places where they could help and failure to protect the artillery and use it effectively precipitated massive British confusion. Low levels of experience and discipline within the ranks did not allow Braddock to iron out the initial confusion and reestablish a coherent fighting force. As a result, and as if to underscore the lack of discipline among the troops, panic eventually ensued and a frantic retreat began for the river.[55] With pride and a hint of anger, one survivor noted, "[e]very Man was alert, did all we could, but the Men dropped like Leaves in Autumn, all was Confusion, and in Spight of what the Officers and bravest of the Men could do, Numbers run away, nay fired on us, that would have forced them to rally."[56]

The men and officers kept running, however, all the way to Philadelphia and eventually New York. In a little over two hours of fighting, the French, Canadians, and Indians had expelled the mighty British forces from all colonies south of New York. In Pennsylvania, it now turned to the traditionally pacific provincial government to do what the king had not—defeat France and its irregulars.

CHAPTER 4

"This Unfortunate and Unexpected Change in our Affairs"

After General Edward Braddock's disastrous defeat in the summer of 1755, the British army removed itself from the colonial frontier. The shattered command first moved towards Philadelphia, and ultimately ended up in New York. Following closely on the army's heels, French, Canadian, and Indian raiders attacked British colonial settlements with a deadly efficiency. In response to such dangers and fearing for their lives, many settlers quit the borderlands and began an exodus for the east. Eventually, few settlements remained west of the Susquehanna River. In such a situation, Pennsylvania and its southern neighbors found themselves alone against France and its allies until British forces once again returned in the spring of 1758.

Pennsylvania itself proved woefully unprepared for the struggle. Traditional Quaker leadership had disallowed military development in the colony's seventy-year history. Moreover, longstanding peaceful relationships with local Indian peoples

reinforced Pennsylvania's negligence of defensive measures.
Finally, remoteness from the French to the north before their
arrival in the Ohio country and the distance from the Spanish to
the south had long kept the colony protected from imperial
struggles.[1] As late as King George's War in the 1740s,
Pennsylvanians remained largely indifferent to military
preparation. When Ohio Indians under the leadership of Scaroudy
arrived in Philadelphia on November 13, 1747, they asked colonial
leaders to "put more Fire under your Kettle."[2] In response to the
request, the provincials provided some material support but
contributed only a few volunteer companies to battle the French
forces. Pennsylvania's natural pacifism and geographical location
had therefore never required local military units. As a result, the
Quaker Colony had no active government fortifications, public
armories, or military institutions in the fall of 1755.[3] Governor
Robert Hunter Morris quickly identified his colony's
defenselessness, informing the assembly:

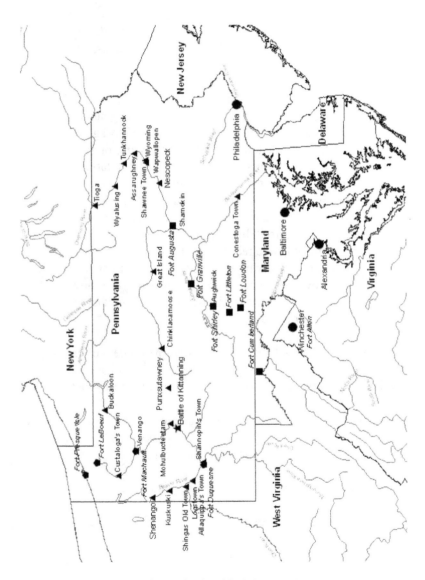

Map 3: The state of Pennsylvania and its defenses in 1756.

"This unfortunate and unexpected change in our affairs [referring to Braddock's defeat] deeply affects every one of his Majesty's Colonies, but none of them in so sensible a manner as this province; while having no militia it is hereby left exposed to the cruel incursions of the French and barbarous Indians, who delight in shedding human blood, and who made no distinction as to age or sex; to those that are armed against them, or such as they can surprise in their peaceful habitations, all are alike the objects of their cruelty—slaughtering the tender infant and frightened mother, with equal joy and fierceness. To such enemies, spurred by the native cruelty of their tempers, encouraged by their late success, and having now no army to fear, are the inhabitants of this province exposed; and by such may we now expect to be overrun, if we do not immediately prepare for our own defence."[4]

The government then began the cumbersome process of creating a military complex from scratch. Eventually, two militia acts passed the assembly, three provincial battalions formed, and numerous forts were constructed. Four forts rose west of the Susquehanna River with one battalion under the command of Colonel John Armstrong assigned to defend them. To fill the void before such units and forts could be assembled, private citizens such as frontier notables George Croghan, Andrew Montour, and Conrad Weiser stepped in.[5]

Croghan and Montour raised volunteer companies composed of traders and Indians. Weiser raised several hundred Bucks County farmers; many of them arrived with no better weapons than pitchforks and axes. Expecting the French to follow up on their victory against Braddock, this motley army rushed to Harris' Ferry on the Susquehanna River to block any advance into eastern Pennsylvania. When the attack never materialized, the men returned home. A loose defensive perimeter consequently coalesced along the inhabited fringe of the colony. West of the Susquehanna, few settlements remained and Armstrong's battalion of Pennsylvania provincials settled into garrison duty at forts Loudon, Lyttleton, Granville, and George. Despite the best efforts of both the provincials and private citizens, however, perhaps 923 people had been killed or captured by hostile war parties by the end of 1756.[6]

As raids swept over the frontier of Pennsylvania, several significant, though not decisive, events occurred. Around April 1, a small private stockade named McCord's Fort fell to the Indians. All twenty-seven of its occupants either died or became captives. Three parties pursued the perpetrators, and one caught up to them at Sideling Hill. In a two-hour engagement, in which several participants reported firing an incredible twenty-four rounds apiece, twenty men died and twelve received wounds. Among the dead lay the commanding officer, Captain Alex Culbertson. Only one Indian had been killed at the fort and three in the engagement at Sideling Hill.[7]

Then, on July 22, sixty Indians appeared outside the gates of the government fort named Granville and demanded the garrison present itself for battle. A veteran of George Washington's 1754 expedition, Captain Edward Ward wisely declined the offer and remained inside the stockade. When the attackers appeared to break up and scatter, however, the captain took roughly half the garrison of fifty men and marched east to protect harvesters. His subordinate, Lieutenant Edward Armstrong, consequently found himself under siege when the Indians returned several days later. The warriors proceeded to set the fort on fire, and when the lieutenant attempted to extinguish the flames, he fell dead from a musket ball. His death precipitated a hasty surrender by the survivors.[8]

Largely in response to the fall of Fort Granville, Edward Armstrong's older brother, Colonel John Armstrong, launched a retaliatory raid against the Indian stronghold of Kittanning in September. With three hundred men, the colonel marched several hundred miles and sprung a surprise attack on the village on the morning of September 9. The results proved ambiguous. Armstrong's force burned part of the village to the ground, killed approximately twelve Indians, and recovered perhaps eleven prisoners. On the other hand, the Indians inflicted forty casualties, among them Armstrong, and obliged the attackers to abandon the town in disarray.[9]

The lack of decisive encounters in 1756, however, does not diminish the year's importance as a significant case study. If irregular tactics had not been the deciding factor in the previous two campaigns under George Washington in 1754, and Edward Braddock in 1755; and, they certainly did not succeed in the subsequent expeditions that ultimately conquered the Ohio country in 1758 and 1763, then 1756 allows a unique glimpse at the other reasons for victory or defeat on the frontier. British regulars had withdrawn out of the arena, and French regulars largely remained in garrison at Fort Duquesne. The development of exclusive conflict between British and French irregulars in 1756 should therefore allow the pinpointing of successful ingredients for frontier warfare.

When the conflict of 1756 is examined, therefore, one difference between the French and British irregulars stands out—experience. Whereas the Canadian and Indian lifestyles, raising, and everyday experience often led to familiarity with firearms and forest settings, British colonial culture often did not. The evidence tends to suggest Pennsylvanians engaged in combat with French irregulars on the frontier in 1756 did not possess the same skills and knowledge as their enemies.

Despite conventional and popular belief, firearms appear to have been less prevalent in Pennsylvania in the mid-eighteenth century than generally believed. Returning to the Croghan, Montour, and Weiser forces, it seems interesting to note that many of the men arrived ready to battle the French armed only with pitchforks and axes. The French, after all, had recently defeated General Braddock's ostensibly invincible force. The lack of firearms amongst the rag-tag Pennsylvania army thus indicates a severe shortage.[10]

Contemporary newspaper ads tend to confirm the early scarcity in arms. Beginning on April 10, 1755, private shipments of arms began arriving in Philadelphia, as evidenced by the advertisements in *The Pennsylvania Gazette*. No similar advertisement appeared in the paper since 1748. It can thus be assumed that traders and local production satiated demand in the interwar years. This large spike in arms sales beginning in 1755 and continuing throughout the Seven Years' War suggests that the people of Pennsylvania had begun arming themselves. The need to arm oneself, however, would have been unnecessary if the possession of firearms already represented the norm.[11]

The requirements included in the second Militia Law of Pennsylvania, passed in May of 1756, further demonstrate the lack of usable firearms in the colony at the beginning of the conflict. Among other items, the law insisted that every man between seventeen and fifty "provide himself with one well fixed Muscat, or Fuses [probably meaning 'fusil'], with a worm and Priming Wine."[12] Those deemed too poor to purchase arms received funds from their militia company from which they might arm themselves. This law, first requiring and then providing for the arming of Pennsylvania citizens, strongly supports the idea of a pre-war scarcity of weapons. Such a measure would have been unnecessary with an already well-supplied populace.[13] Thomas Barton, an Anglican minister on the frontier, understood the dire straits of most border settlers. "Not a man in ten," noted Barton,

"is able to purchase a gun."[14] The idea of poorly armed

Pennsylvanians continues to appear during General John Forbes'

subsequent 1758 campaign, where fully two thirds of the

provincials arrived unarmed.[15] Inexperience with firearms directly

translated into inexperience as warriors, and such a detrimental

condition was further exacerbated by inexperience with warfare in

general.

Pennsylvania had never been in a war, and it thus lacked

military institutions and trained soldiers and leaders. Experience

in the colony could only exist from transplants—those who

immigrated from Europe and other colonies and tasted combat in

those areas. Such numbers remained low. "Had the British king

attempted to enslave us before Braddock's War [the Seven Years'

War]," argued Pennsylvanian James Smith, "in all probability he

might readily have done it, because, except the New Englanders,

who had formerly been engaged in war with the Indians, we were

unacquainted with any kind of war."[16] Berks County leaders agreed, complaining to Philadelphia, "we have...no officers

practiced in war."[17] From the pens of Pennsylvanians themselves,

therefore, experience in warfare remained rare, and it proved a

tremendous concern. Combined with little knowledge of weapons,

it comes as no surprise that the colony's military forces fared

poorly in the year's irregular combat.

In the winter of 1755-1756, the Pennsylvania government

built forts Shirley, George, Granville, and Loudon. They

represented the government's presence west of the Susquehanna

River. Governor Morris took great pride in his efforts, writing to

William Shirley in Massachusetts on February 9, 1756:

> "[Fort Shirley] stands near the great path used by
> the Indians and traders, to and from the Ohio, and
> consequently the easiest way of access for the
> Indians into the settlements of this
> Province...This fort [Lyttleton] will not only
> protect the inhabitants in that part of the Province,
> but being upon a road that within a few miles
> joins General Braddocks road, it will prevent the
> march of any regulars into the Province and at the
> same time serve as an advance post or magazine
> in case of an attempt to the westward. For these
> reasons I have caused it to be built in a regular
> form, so that it may, in a little time and at a small

expense, be so strengthened as to hold out against cannon."[18]

Apparently, the governor expected plenty of foreknowledge of a French attack, because other assessments of the forts proved disparaging. The French noted that the English "construct several pretended forts; that is to say to enclose a number of dwellings of stockades."[19] Even General Forbes, upon arriving in 1758, found the forts significantly lacking.[20] No matter how well built, the bottom line remained—the forts proved as useful in stopping irregular raiding parties as an island might be at stopping a mighty fleet. In light of this reality, however, the governor had a plan.

The plan required seventy-five man garrisons in each of the four forts west of the Susquehanna River. While leaving enough strength to guard the forts, the troops were ordered to range or patrol the woods in either direction. In this way, the governor hoped to intercept French raiding parties before they hit the settlements. Apparently, Morris truly believed the rangers would be effective.[21] On at least one occasion, he berated Major James Burd because "the Indians who committed those last murders must have passed near where ye Fort was order'd to be built."[22] The French, however, already knew what the governor did not—the plan contained flaws. "In vain," stated a French dispatch, "did these provinces which have no Indians to aid them, levy and pay a thousand men, at the opening of this campaign, who dressed and painted themselves in the Indian fashion; in vain did they send them to scour the woods."[23] Indeed, in vain did Morris order provincial scouts to match skills with French and Indian irregulars on the frontiers of Pennsylvania. The failure of British rangers in 1756, moreover, can be attributed to the overwhelming inexperience of the troops.

Similar to some of the red-coated soldiers in General Braddock's army of a year before, putting on the green military jacket of the Pennsylvania provincial forces did not necessarily make one a trained, experienced soldier. On April 18, 1756, Captain Hugh Mercer lamented to Morris, "I am sorry to observe that numbers of our best men have declined the service."[24] Another officer, Captain Joseph Shippen, had an even more scathing impression of his troops. "If we attempt to personate soldiers in the field," he wrote, "we shall soon be hissed off the military stage…[having only]…raw men unacquainted with discipline and obedience to command."[25] Some of the inexperience of the troops could be attributed to the government itself. Although the governor pushed for long enlistments, Pennsylvania's assembly believed many soldiers would reenlist and initially allowed three, six, and twelve month enlistments. As a result, when many men failed to rejoin, the experience they had gained in service was squandered when they returned home. The provincial units thus required the continuous enlistment of raw troops.[26]

The type of Pennsylvanian that typically enlisted, moreover, ensured that the provincial forces would be inadequately experienced with firearms and wilderness experience. A twentieth century historian wrote romantically of the men, claiming, "[e]very man was a frontiersman, large and sinewy, toughened by hardships in the forests, and a dead shot."[27]

Unfortunately for the colony, this description does not accurately apply to the bulk of the provincial soldiers. Instead of the "frontiersman" who had been "toughened by hardships in the forests," more than sixty percent of the troops had been laborers and tradesmen before enlisting. Both economic and geographical factors would have made these men among the most unlikely in Pennsylvania to have substantial experience with firearms and the wilderness. Furthermore, more than seventy-five percent of recruits came from the recent immigrant population.[28] A Philadelphian merchant named Joseph Turner noted:

> "Almost all the Pallentines who came in familys could no be Disposed off, none cared to be encumbered with them for breeding women brought charges to a family more than the Husband Earn'd[.] many such family were suffer'd to go into the back parts on their own Security who now…are undone & some of them from any thing we know are in a Starving condition. Hardly able to maintain themselves…the Husbands have lately Enlisted."[29]

Here, poverty appears to have made immigrants a common target for recruitment. Although necessity may have forced immigrants onto the frontiers, that same poverty suggests that they too represented the most unlikely of Pennsylvanians to have owned and gained experience with firearms. With these types of men expected to enact Governor Morris' defensive strategy, it comes as no surprise that French irregulars easily passed by the forts with their ranger battalions and wrought havoc amid the settlements.

The settlers proved just as unable to locate and defeat French irregulars as the provincial forces. Infrequently, they did manage to beat back attacks. According to *The Pennsylvania Gazette*, "an Indian came to the House of Philip Robinson…carrying a green Bush before him; but being discovered he got safe off, tho' fired at by said Robinson."[30] Although the astute Robinson's ability to identify a moving bush as unnatural seems noteworthy, Pennsylvanian settlers tended more often to be reactionary. Instead of preventing or destroying raiding parties, pioneers managed to respond. In exasperation, Governor Morris wrote Virginia Governor Robert Dinwiddie that Indians quit the area and simply raided elsewhere when confronted with armed defenders. As a result, militia soldiers often vainly pursued attackers, and this typically meant they followed a trail of destruction.[31]

Primarily as gravediggers, rather than avenging soldiers, many Pennsylvania settlers followed the trails of the raiding parties that had killed and captured their friends, families, and neighbors. In November 1756, Captain Jacob Morgan set out "to get Intelligence of the Mischief done at Tolheo, or thereabouts, and to get a Number of Men to join them to go and seek for the Persons who were scalped by the Indians, and to help, in the best Manner they could, the poor distressed Inhabitants."[32] Although on a noble, humanitarian mission, Morgan's goals underscore the lack of skill amongst Pennsylvanians. Instead of catching and punishing the attackers, he set out to clean up after them. While following the path of the raiding party, Morgan and his men found and buried ten people at seven different locations. One of the dead, Caspar Spring, had his "[b]rains…beat out…two cuts in his Breasts, shot in the Back, and otherwise cruelly used, which a Regard to Decency forbids mentioning."[33] Another, named

Beslinger, remained with his "[b]rains beat out, his Mouth much mangled, one of his Eyes cut out, and one of his Ears gashed, and had two Knives lying on his Breasts." Such scenes, and the inability of settlers to do anything other than bury the dead, appear common.

On another occasion, local citizens again followed the path of a particularly destructive raiding party. They arrived at a private fort named Coombes, where they found "only four Men in this Fort, two of which were unable to bear Arms; but upwards of forty Women and Children, who were in a very poor Situation, being afraid to go out of the Fort, even for a Drink of Water."[34] Although this account unfortunately does not indicate why the two men could not carry arms, it does emphasize Pennsylvanians' inability to deal with enemy irregulars in the woods. Not only did the tracking party not catch the perpetrators, the settlers in the fort had been unable to retrieve water for fear of an ambush.

The incident at Sideling Hill appears to be the only major occasion that settlers managed to successfully pursue attacking irregulars. Even in this case, however, the success appears to be more the product of luck than skill. Three parties set out to find the raiders, and only one came across them. With numerous prisoners, the attackers should have been slower and less able to conceal their tracks. In that regard, it seems surprising that only one out of three of the Pennsylvania parties located them. The results of the conflict further exemplify the advantage of skill and experience French irregulars had over their British counterparts. The two-hour engagement cost the Pennsylvanians twenty deaths and twelve wounded. According prisoner John Cox, who later escaped, the colonists managed to kill only four on the other side. Thus, out of Captain Alex Culbertson's fifty-man force, which claimed to have shot twenty-four rounds apiece, an estimated 1,200 rounds managed to kill four people. It does not seem to represent a field day for marksmanship. To make matters worse, Cox later reported that one of the four dead had been one of the very prisoners Culbertson attempted to rescue.[35] In retrospect, then, the battle of Sideling Hill appears a fine example of French irregular superiority. Two additional examples, concerning the provincial forces, reinforce this conclusion.

On July 30, Fort Granville fell to a party of sixty French, Canadian, and Indian raiders. Here, Pennsylvania provincials possessed a clear advantage inside a stockade. Because irregulars traditionally had little success against fortifications, the event appears even more remarkable. Part of the fort's downfall resulted simply from its location. Perched along the Juniata River, French irregulars managed to sneak close enough to launch burning pine knots against the walls. In a wooden stockade, the Pennsylvania forces should have had preexisting plans for combating fire. Indeed, Edward Armstrong's efforts to extinguish the flames suggests that a strong effort had been made. However, once the lieutenant fell mortally wounded, the garrison lost its nerve and surrendered. With experienced, disciplined troops, such a result should have been avoidable against irregular attackers.[36]

Then, Colonel Armstrong's raid on Kittanning in September further identified failures with Pennsylvanians' woodland skills. Six pilots, including Thomas Burke and James Chalmers, had been hired in addition to rangers to guide the army to its destination. Failures by these men seriously compromised Armstrong's mission. Upon the army's march towards the village, soldiers spotted a campfire. After an inquiry, the colonel's spies informed him that three or four Indians camped near the flames. Detouring the main army around the fire, the colonel left twelve men with orders to attack the camp at dawn. When the soldiers made their attack, they found more than twenty Indians opposing them. Either wiped out or forced to flee, the soldiers had suffered terribly from the spies' misinformation.[37]

A short distance away, Armstrong had broken his army into two columns. One would attack the village directly while the other would hook around a ridge to the right. The latter apparently got lost and never entered the battle.[38] In his post-battle report, the colonel claimed, "rather than by the Pilots we were guided by the beating of the Drum and the Whooping of the Warriors at their Dance."[39] How one wing could hear the noise but the other could not remains a mystery, but the events at Kittanning ultimately led Armstrong to a startling conclusion.

In his post-battle report, the colonel cast doubt upon the abilities of his woodsmen. Blaming them for his limited success, he wrote, "the Ignorance of our Pilots who neither know the true Situation of the Town nor the best Paths that lead thereto."[40] "It appear'd they had not been nigh enough the Town," he went on, "either to perceive the true Situation of it, the Number of the Enemy, or what Way it might most advantageously attack'd."[41] In short, Armstrong believed his scouts had not gone anywhere near the town. Interestingly, this same conclusion came to Colonel Henry Bouquet and General John Forbes almost two years later when they too doubted his scouts.

The evidence of Pennsylvania's overall failure was evident. Colonel Armstrong indicated to the governor that the government forts could not protect the citizens, warning him, "the new settlements being all fled except Shearman's Valley, whom (if God do not preserve we fear will suffer very soon."[42] In York

County, where three thousand people had once resided, less than one hundred remained. Finally, by August 19, the Juniata and Shearman Valleys had been deserted.[43] Pennsylvanians had lost faith in their government's ability to defeat French irregulars, and could not cope with them either. Joseph Mayhew, a Conococheague Valley settler, put it best:

> "We are in the greatest Distress here. Besides the Danger we are exposed to, and the Shortness of our Crops, we are now full of People, who have been obliged to leave their Plantations, to avoid falling into the Hands of the Savages. Poor as we are, we can rescue a little Part of our poor Stock to our Fellow Subjects, who are reduced to begging their Bread. Last Friday the Indians killed three Men in the Gap of the Mountain; and we have certain Accounts that there is a large Body, who, we expect, will fall upon this Settlement. This Day we have an Account that 3 or 4 Persons have been killed by the Savages near the Line. We donknow what to do; hard to give up our Livings, and yet, unless we are assisted, that will be the best we are to expect. The people about ten or twelve Miles beyond us have left their Plantations upon this Alarm. JOSEPH MAYHEW."[44]

Pennsylvania as a whole, both as a government and as a people, had been woefully under experienced in warfare, firearms, and the wilderness to even come close to matching the French irregulars.

Although French successes in 1756 represented a tactical victory, strategically the year had little effect on the eventual outcome of victory in the Ohio country. Already in possession of territory they were interested in, French harassment techniques attempted to keep the British off-balance and unable to launch a new expedition against Fort Duquesne. The British, however, committed themselves to conquering the major French citadels.[45] Thus, by the spring of 1758 British regulars once again massed in eastern Pennsylvania for a third attempt to capture the forks. By failing to knock the colonists out of the war with their overwhelming superiority in woodland experience, the French irregulars had simply provided a training ground for British irregulars that ultimately accompanied their regular counterparts in 1758.

CHAPTER 5

"Necessity Will Turn Me a Cherokee"

In the spring of 1758, the British military attempted once more to expel France from its defensive position at Fort Duquesne in the Ohio country. Upon assuming command of the expedition, General John Forbes exclaimed, "necessity will turn me a Cherokee, and don't be surprised if I take F: du Quesne at the head of them; and them only, For to this day I have no orders to command any troops."[1] Although the idea of Forbes, sick with an intestinal disorder, being carried to Fort Duquesne in a litter by nearly naked Indians seems absurd, the prospect seemed very real to him. Colonial assemblies quarreled about troop commitments and British regulars assigned to the campaign had yet to sail north from South Carolina. Eventually, however, his army began to form. By the summer, the general commanded the First Highland Battalion, several companies of the Royal American Regiment, three battalions of the Pennsylvania Regiment, two Virginian regiments, and small detachments from Maryland, Delaware, and

North Carolina. Small parties of Cherokee and Catawba warriors from the south also arrived.[2]

Using several of the forts built by Pennsylvania in the previous years as bases, Forbes set out towards Fort Duquesne. Although he vacillated between using Edward Braddock's southern route from Virginia and cutting a new road from Pennsylvania for much of the summer, the general planned to at least travel through Pennsylvania to Raystown. Here, the Redcoats paused to build Fort Bedford. Ultimately, Forbes elected to continue his road directly to Fort Duquesne from Raystown, thus opting to ignore Braddock's road and creating much consternation amongst the southern soldiers in his command. Along the length of Forbes' new road, forts had been built approximately every fifty miles. Among them, Fort Ligonier arose only fifty miles from the British objective on the Ohio. To further strengthen his supply and communication route, the general ordered fortified camps constructed in between the major outposts. Thus, British troops

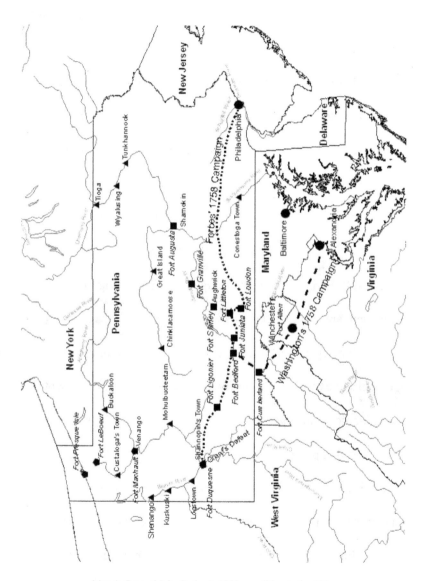

Map 4: General John Forbes's 1758 expedition to the Ohio.

possessed the luxury of relatively safe locations at the end of most marches.

During this time, Captain Francois-Marie Le Marchand de Lignery waited at Fort Duquesne with his heavily outnumbered force. Not content to merely sit back and wait for Forbes' army to arrive, Lignery decided upon a strategy of launching raid after raid at the advancing British. If the raids proved strong enough, the captain might even be able to bog the attackers down until winter. As a result, Forbes advanced through sporadic raiding by French, Canadian, and Indian irregulars.[3]

By September of 1758, troops under the command of Colonel James Burd of Pennsylvania reached the site of present day Ligonier, and began construction of the fort by the same name. At that point, the expedition nearly came undone. Colonel Henry Bouquet of the Royal American Regiment, Forbes' second in command and the man who ran many of the army's operations for the ailing general, sent several hundred men under Major James Grant of the Highlanders to reconnoiter Fort Duquesne in force. On the evening of September 13, Grant and his force reached a hill overlooking the fort. In the morning, he broke up his troops, forming some on the hill, leaving some in the rear, and sending the rest to burn several of the buildings outside the French defenses. Upon learning of the attack, French irregulars swarmed out of the fort and the surrounding area and vigorously attacked Grant and his men. The results proved disastrous for the Redcoats. Nearly one half of the British force wound up killed or captured, with Colonel Grant among the captured. As the survivors returned to Fort Ligonier, however, no panic prevailed as it had at the Great Meadows after Edward Braddock's defeat at the Monongahela in 1755. Forbes' army simply absorbed the losses and continued on.[4]

Then, on October 12, the French launched a similar attack on the British at Fort Ligonier. Initially, the action went well for the French. Unaware of the danger, many British troops had been caught outside the fort in the open. As the tide of battle went against his men, Colonel Burd dispatched reinforcements. They

proved unable, however, to push the French back, and all
survivors ultimately worked their way back into the fortifications.
At that point, the French irregulars placed the fort under a daylong
siege. Depending upon surprise, Lignery had not dispatched
artillery to support his troops. As most of the British soldiers had
found safety inside Ligonier's walls, and they had support from
mortars, the French irregulars eventually conceded defeat and
retreated westward. Although the French ploy to defeat the British
failed, it resulted in sixty-four more killed, wounded, or missing
British troops.[5]

As the season advanced, however, Lignery's delaying
actions appeared to have born fruit. Forbes' army, strung out over
hundreds of miles of Pennsylvania wilderness, seemed stalled at
Fort Ligonier—a mere fifty miles from its destination. The
general consequently concluded that the campaign could not be
completed that year—it would have to be resumed in the spring.

During the lull after the October 12 battle, a small party of
provincials scouted the area surrounding Fort Ligonier. Close

enough to the fort to be heard, a party of French irregulars ambushed the party, and Colonel George Washington personally led a relief force. Unbeknownst to the colonel, the scouting party had already forced the ambushers to withdraw. Hearing the approach of Washington's party, the scouts concluded that the French had circled around to their rear and mistakenly fired on their compatriots when they arrived. In the confusion, the colonel's men quickly returned fire. Washington realized the mistake, and stepped in front of his men, knocking their weapons skyward with his sword. When the firing finally stopped, forty provincial troops lay dead, though the colonel miraculously escaped unharmed.[6]

Despite Forbes' decision to postpone completing the campaign until the spring of 1759, timely intelligence changed his mind. The French at Fort Duquesne remained in poor shape, and had been abandoned by their Canadian and Indian irregulars due to the failure of the attack on Fort Ligonier and the lateness of the season. In addition, the Pennsylvania Quakers had initiated peace negotiations with the disaffected tribes. The French position appeared ripe for the plucking, and Forbes' slow moving army thus ultimately proved beneficial. The general quickly formed several columns, and marched for the Ohio River. As the British neared the fortification, they saw smoke on the horizon and heard loud explosions. On November 24, advance troops discovered the source—the French had abandoned and burned their post, retreating down the Ohio River to Illinois and up the Allegheny River to the smaller stockades in that area.[7]

Thus, Forbes succeeded where two preceding commanders had failed. Like those before him, the general faced continuous harassment from French irregulars and relied upon small numbers of allied Indian and generally ineffective colonial irregulars to counter them. He had also absorbed a seriously lopsided defeat, without allowing the remainder of his force to panic. Ultimately, success attended Forbes' efforts because he shielded and protected his regulars by applying them where they were best in the wilderness—behind fortifications.

According to the British battle plan, and perhaps due to supply issues, units remained separated for much of the summer and fall. For hundreds of miles in Pennsylvania, Maryland, and Virginia, soldiers maintained garrisons and provided escorts. French irregulars thus found numerous opportunities for small-scale actions. In addition, the British irregulars often conducted scouting missions. The nearly six months encompassing the Forbes expedition thus proved a highly active period for irregulars for both sides, where they served several functions.

Primarily, British irregulars provided intelligence gathering for the regular army trailing behind. "I need not recommend," wrote Bouquet to his superior, "the endeavoring to get Intelligence of Fort du quesne, and the strength if [of] the ennemy in those posts, and by all means to have the road reconnoitred from Rayes town to the Yohageny."[8] Although most of the scouts focused on the Fort Duquesne area, Forbes dispatched multiple parties, shrouded in secrecy, to scout and raid the Venango area along France's supply lines.[9] According to

Forbes, the intelligence gathering scouts would fill the "necessity for some good guides to attend us."[10]

Irregulars also performed escort duty for provision caravans. Early in the campaign, Forbes notified his superior, General Abercromby, "I assemble the rest of our provincialls all along the road from Lancaster to Raes town to serve as escorts &c. to the provisions."[11] As reported by *The Pennsylvania Gazette*, escorting service could be very dangerous work. "The Escort," it stated, "consisting of fourteen Men, under the Command of Lieutenant Hayes, in their Return unfortunately fell in with a large Party of French and Indians…but our People were overpowered by Numbers, and the Lieutenant, and four Men killed, five were made Prisoners, and the other five escaped."[12] To partially alleviate supply problems, and thus lessen the need for escorts, British irregulars often received permission to hunt. The activity, however, often led to soldiers getting lost in the woods.[13]

Finally, Forbes' irregular troops drew the task of playing a deadly cat-and-mouse game with their French counterparts. The army's large size required tremendous amounts of food for survival. Due to the lack of wagons, and the popularity of fresh meat over salted rations, a large number of live beef cattle accompanied the army on its westward march. Combined with the army's horses, these animals consumed enormous portions of fodder. The forested nature of the army's path provided few natural meadows in which to release the cattle and horses. The inability of the scarce wagons to spare much space for feed exacerbated the shortages. As a result, the British often found they could only release the animals into the woods to find their own sustenance.[14] Bouquet, in a letter to Colonel Jeffrey Amherst, explained the problem with this method. "Being obliged to have our cattle and our horses in the woods," he wrote, "our people could not guard or search for them without being continually liable to fall into the hands of the enemy."[15]

Worse yet, raids that the French irregulars had undertaken in the fall of 1755 had not abated in Pennsylvania by 1758. On the frontier, and even well east of the Susquehanna River, attacks continued.[16] At Lancaster and Carlisle, "they [French irregulars] are scalping every day and have broke up all the settlements in that neighborhood."[17] To protect both his own men and the remaining settlements of Pennsylvania, Forbes found himself obliged to commit large numbers of his men to chasing the French through the woods.

The soldiers assigned to this hazardous duty tried a variety of techniques, typically with little success. At times, they set up roadblocks on all known pathways, hoping to catch raiders on their return westward.[18] As Pennsylvanians had found in 1756, stationary defenses often proved ineffective. Thus, at other times, Forbes' men vainly chased their enemies through the woods. Forbes penned his mounting frustration to Philadelphian Richard Peters. "I hope we have chaced off the Enemy Indians from this neighborhood," he wrote, "having had 300 Highlanders with all the best woodsmen out…but never could have the Good fortune of falling on with any of them."[19] On another occasion, he informed Peters, "two of the Indians fired upon the Head of a party of ours of 80 men, yet notwithstanding they were Instantaneously pursued they gott away."[20] Forbes' disappointment with his irregulars' inability to deal with their enemy counterparts, however, did not match the frustration their scouting abilities caused him.

Similar to Armstrong's Kittanning Raid of 1756, the failure of British intelligence gathering sources appears a common theme throughout the Forbes Expedition. Numerous parties, dispatched to ascertain the French positions and strength, proved disappointing.[21] Forbes complained to Abercromby, "I can learn little or nothing of their [French] state at Fort Du Quesne, notwithstanding the numberless partys I have sent out."[22] To clarify some of the difficulties, however, the general offered an explanation to Secretary of State William Pitt. "I have now about 400 Men out upon scouting partys," he wrote, "but as they have four or five Hundred miles in the going and returning, what Intelligence they bring is always of so old a date that there is no trusting to it."[23] Whatever the reasons, Forbes thus suffered as a result of the chronic issues with British irregulars that his predecessors had.

Much of Forbes' difficulties arose from the state of the irregulars themselves. Initially, the general could draw upon both Indian allies from the south as well as provincials. The Indian allies proved a mixed blessing. At the outset, they arrived in large numbers and Forbes found them more than satisfactory. "The Cherokee and Catauba Indians," he wrote, "have been fully as good as their promise."[24] Scouting parties brought in intelligence, scalps, and prisoners. As time went on, however, numbers began to decline and with them went much of the esteem they originally held with the British. By the time Fort Duquesne fell, only a handful remained.[25] Some enjoyed seeing the Indians leave because, according to Major Joseph Shippen, "it seems little dependence can be put on any of them [Indians]."[26] Indeed, Indian irregulars had presented the British with a variety of unique difficulties of their own.

On the one hand, British officers found themselves at a loss when dealing with allied Indians. Forbes discovered that they could be "capable of being led away upon any caprice or whime that seizes them, I am obliged by every Artifice to amuse them from returning home."[27] In order to prevent the natural "caprice" and "whim" of the Indians from taking them south, British officers most often attempted to keep them busy.[28]

In action as well, however, Indians posed difficulties. When in the woods, allied and enemy Indians often proved indistinguishable to jumpy provincial scouts and soldiers. As a result of several incidents, Forbes found that "the Cherokees ought to have Signals to know Each other by to prevent Mischieff."[29] Eventually, he decided upon yellow bands, and further mistakes seemed to stop. Fortunately for the general, it appears that on no occasions did enemy Indians utilize yellow bands as a ploy to get near British troops.

Finally, Indian culture and warfare methods proved eminently frustrating for their British allies. Although the Indians often proved successful as scouts, the allied British often found it difficult to remove prisoners from native possession. As a result, interrogation of prisoners, one way to remedy Forbes' intelligence deficiencies, proved impossible.[30] Despite the difficulties of dealing with Indians, provincial irregulars often did not offer a better option for the general.

By 1758, some provincial soldiers in Forbes' army had accrued experience in wilderness warfare. Colonels John Armstrong and James Burd, both battalion commanders in the Pennsylvania Regiment, had commanded men for several years on the Pennsylvania frontier. Colonel George Washington had not only served on the two prior campaigns but had also commanded Virginia's troops on the frontier since Braddock's defeat. Consequently, the colonel once argued that his men, through long experience, equaled any in the woods. Then, when a particularly experienced group of Maryland rangers set out to leave when their enlistments ran out, Forbes acted quickly to retain them with the King's gold. Out of these experienced units, irregular forces organized, typically possessing two officers, one sergeant, one corporal, and twenty-five privates.[31]

Early in the campaign, steps began to further improve the provincials' ability to act as irregulars. The troops trained to aim their fire, take advantageous positions, to load lying behind logs, and to fight on the move. Many received horses in order to greatly improve their mobility. Finally, numbers of provincials removed their European uniforms and adopted the Indian dress. Both Forbes and Bouquet actively supported their subordinates making such alterations. To that end, all skins brought in by hunters became moccasins and leggings for those troops. At Fort Cumberland in Maryland, initially not knowing Forbes' open-mindedness, Colonel Washington proceeded upon his own authority to dress his men as Indians. One of his best rangers, Lieutenant Colby Chew, stripped to only a breechclout and moccasins. Timidly, Washington then dispatched some of his dressed-down men to Bouquet at Fort Bedford. To his relief, he soon found Bouquet in complete agreement.[32] "It gives me great pleasure," wrote Washington to one of his officers, "to find this Dress; or undress as you justly remark; so pleasing to Colo. Bouquet."[33] With such measures being widely adopted, Forbes' irregulars improved their ability to function in the wilderness.

Yet, despite these improvements British commanders continued to denigrate the abilities of their colonial irregulars. Indicating a lack of confidence, on almost every occasion they desired Indians to go with their own scouting parties.[34] "I beg you will gett some brisk officers from among the provincialls," Forbes instructed Bouquet, "to try some scouting partys with a good many Indians along with them."[35]Furthermore, Forbes and Bouquet's support of Indian dress did not result from their respect for its functional ability. Instead, they adopted it for its deceptive qualities. Forbes wanted "to make Indians of Par of our provincial soldiers."[36] "I was resolved," he went on, "upon getting some of the best people in every Corps to go out Scouting in that stile, for as you justly observe, the Shadow may be often taken for the reality."[37] In the statement, Forbes betrayed his lack of confidence in colonial irregulars. The French did not fear them, and he consequently decided to use them deceptively, to make the enemy believe he possessed more Indian irregulars than he actually did.

Thus, British disrespect for colonial abilities in the woods continued. Captain Ourry considered them raw and worthless.[38] Forbes, for his part, wrote to his superior, "I have not so many [regulars] as to keep my irregulars in due decency and order."[39] He desperately wanted large numbers of regulars for his campaign. "Send me what you may think proper of regular troops," he continued, "for at present I can Brag of none, notwithstanding I am very well inclin'd to think favorably, and even partially of the Highlanders and the 4 Companies of Royal Americans."[40] The general eventually received what he had requested, and his overall strategy centered upon their abilities, not those of the irregulars. Incidents such as Washington's friendly fire encounter further eroded Forbes' confidence in his provincial troops.[41]

With his strategy hinging upon the skills and abilities of the British regular, Forbes faced a dilemma marching into the wilderness. He could make a quick dash towards Fort Duquesne, as Braddock did, and hope to catch the fort and its irregulars unprepared. Or, as he ultimately chose to do, he could slowly plod forward, stopping to build strong points along the way. Using such a technique, the general would only have to use irregulars to shield his regulars for relatively short marches. According to Bouquet's marching orders, eight men would lead the army followed by a thirteen man advance guard, two pickets composed of thirty-one men walking in two parallel columns, the artillery train, the main body, and the baggage under guard of thirty-two men. Finally, two flanking parties, one to each side of the army would be stationed at the head and rear of the column. To provide the cover, Forbes often relied upon the three hundred-man ranger company of Lieutenant Colonel Dagworthy of Maryland composed primarily of woodsmen from Maryland, Delaware, and North Carolina.[42] So wary did the British army prove to be, that no Braddock style defeat seemed possible and thus the columns never received obstruction of any large body of enemies. "All his motions were narrowly watched by the Enemy," crowed one

Briton after the capture of Fort Duquesne, "who, finding that he

not only proceeded with Care and Circumspection, but with

inflexible Steadiness, and that they could neither face him in the

Field, retard his March, nor resist him in their Fort, retired to their

Batteus, and fell down the River."[43] The skill with which Forbes

handled his army, and the clear benefits provided by numerous

strong points, seem evident in light of the two major encounters of

the campaign.

In September, Colonel Bouquet dispatched Major James

Grant with a large body of men to move towards Fort Duquesne.

Foreshadowing the confusion that followed, Grant determined,

"[t]hat we might the better distinguish our own people every one

had a white shirt over his coat."[44] Taking post on top of a nearby

hill, the major sent troops to burn down the forts outbuildings and

thus draw out the defenders. He further split his forces, leaving

Major Lewis, a provincial, in the rear with another body of men.

Immediately, some of the Virginians got lost. Despite the

confusion and wide dispersal of the British forces, the attack initially went well against the scattered defenders encountered by the raiding party. The tide then turned, as French, Canadian, and Indian reinforcements rushed out of the fort.[45] The original raiding party, composed of three companies of Highlanders, "stood firm a long time, and by their regular platoon firing annoyed the enemy greatly."[46] The survivors eventually retreated to the main body, and Major Lewis also moved forward to join his beleaguered comrades. The confusion created by three separate parties attempting to join together under fire, combined with being surrounded by a numerically superior French force, resulted in the dispersal and flight of the surviving British troops. With the dead lay Colby Chew, the effective Virginian irregular, and Majors Grant and Lewis wound up captured. In all, nearly half the attacking force--270 men--ended up killed or captured. The remainder, however, had the luxury of retreating to a fortified post at Ligonier.[47]

The psychological effect the pallisaded forts built by Forbes had on his men cannot be underestimated. In 1755, the survivors of Braddock's army had no such fortification nearby to seek safety. Instead, they headed for Colonel Dunbar's force trailing behind the main army and therefore not engaged in the battle. Those men, as well, were exposed in the open forest. Panic had quickly spread, and all hopes of mounting a second attempt dissipated. In 1758, however, no such situation occurred. Grant's survivors knew there existed a friendly fort nearby. More importantly, the men garrisoned in the fort felt relatively secure as they viewed the returning stragglers. No widespread panic erupted. As a result, Forbes' army managed to absorb the losses and push on towards their objective. The value of fortifications to an offensive operation further became evident in October.

On October 12, Colonel Bouquet, traveling towards Fort Ligonier, heard the distant noise of battle. What he heard represented the final French attempt to stop Forbes' advance into the Ohio country. Six hundred to twelve hundred French,

Canadians, and Indians began the attack by firing on a small group

of soldiers outside the fort. The British commander, Colonel

James Burd of the Pennsylvania Regiment, quickly dispatched five

hundred men to repel the attack. Although the reinforcement fell

back, Burd had the trump card—fortifications and artillery. Some

British accounts report hearing enemy artillery, but if it existed it

never fired on Ligonier. Instead, Burd managed to withdraw most

of his forces into the fort and defended it effectively with cannon

against three main attacks throughout the day and the subsequent

night.[48] "In return for their most melodious music," wrote Burd,

"we gave them a lesson of shells, which soon made them

retreat."[49] Sixty-four British soldiers ended up killed or wounded,

and French losses remain unknown. The British, for their part,

believed French losses to be high. One wounded soldier, who hid

among the dead throughout the night, reported the French took a

long time in removing their comrades from the field of battle.[50]

Thus, despite the additional losses in men, Forbes' plan for fortifications ultimately proved able to protect his troops from even the largest of French raiding parties.

The very safety the forts provided, however, discouraged the soldiers from pursuing the French after their withdraw. "I shall be very sorry," wrote Forbes to Bouquet, "if they [the French] return unmolested which would show them their superiority over us in their fighting in the woods & give them a boldness that I would willingly crush."[51] To Pitt, Forbes went on, "I was extreamly angry to find our people had not pursued and attack their rear in their retreat, from which we might have made reprizalls, but as our troops were mostly provincialls, I was obliged to attribute it to their ignorance."[52] The soldiers' unwillingness to leave the safety of the fort ultimately allowed their attackers to return home unmolested, but in the end it proved of little consequence. By the time Forbes and his army arrived at the gates of Fort Duquesne more than a month later, the French had left.

Forbes' victory thus resulted from his decision to put his troops where they could function best—behind wooden walls. By protecting his regulars and provincials, he did not place the burden of victory on his irregulars. They made contributions, but did not dictate the outcome. The French, for their part, did put the burden of victory on irregulars. Although they certainly inflicted more casualties on the British than they themselves received, Forbes managed to absorb the losses. Even considering Grant's debacle, the British ultimately succeeded in 1758 because they did not put themselves in a position to receive a catastrophic, demoralizing defeat. Although Forbes' success led to temporary peace in the Ohio country, the defenses he left behind ultimately became critical to any future campaigning in the area.

CHAPTER 6

"Whatever Our Fate May Be"

After General John Forbes' successful capture of Fort

Duquesne in 1758, the French abandoned the Ohio country and in

1760 lost all of its possessions in North America east of the

Mississippi River. Relative peace prevailed until 1763, when

dissatisfied Indian nations of the Great Lakes and Ohio regions

rose up in Pontiac's Uprising. British posts throughout the

frontier, including those in present northwest Pennsylvania, fell to

the Indian warriors. Forts Pitt, Ligonier, and Bedford held out,

despite repeated attacks and sieges. Then, in June, Fort Pitt fell

silent.[53]

Unable to ascertain whether Fort Pitt had fallen or had

been put under a tight siege, British Commander in Chief of North

America, General Jeffrey Amherst, ordered Colonel Henry

Bouquet to its relief. The timing could not have been worse.

Since the end of the Seven Years' War in North America in 1760,

British forces had simultaneously been slimmed down and spread out. Those units that had not been deactivated by the government in London garrisoned the numerous frontier posts Britain inherited from the vanquished French. Many of those men lay dead or had become prisoners of the Indians. Colonial forces had also been largely disbanded, and most colonies proved reluctant to raise troops again so soon after peace had been secured with France. As a result, Bouquet could rely only on small numbers of British regulars recuperating in New York from malaria contracted during service in the Caribbean.[54] After slipping a small number of reinforcements into the posts at Bedford and Ligonier, Bouquet marched with his army. They reached Ligonier on August 2 without any major incidents. After a short pause, the colonel then pushed on towards Fort Pitt.[55] Before leaving, Bouquet wrote Amherst, "[w]e march on the 28th I Shall not write to you before we get to Pittsburgh, unless Something Extraordinary Should happen on the way."[56] On August 5, the extraordinary happened.

As Bouquet's column wound through the woods about halfway between Fort Ligonier and Fort Pitt, Indians rose from the

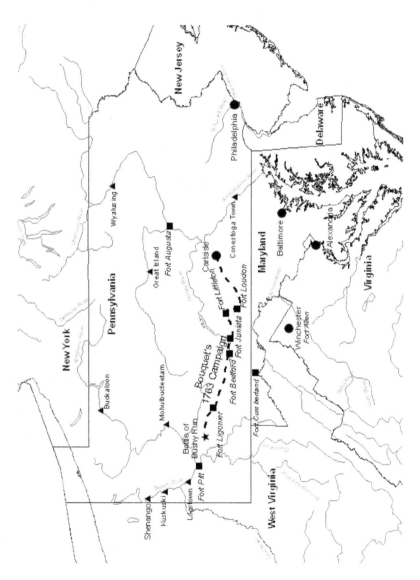

Map 5: Colonel Henry Bouquet's 1763 expedition to the Ohio.

surrounding woods and commenced firing on the Redcoats.

Unlike the disaster that took place at Braddock's defeat, Bouquet's

men did not stay in the valley; but, instead they opted to rush the

hills and dislodge the Indians. Effective as the technique proved,

however, the Indians simply withdrew and went on the attack in

another area. As the fight progressed, the Indians eventually

worked their way to the column's rear and the pack animals. To

protect his supply convoy, Bouquet ordered a retreat, and

established a defensive position on Edge Hill. There, those still

able formed a circular defensive position, laying the wounded in

the center with a fort of flour bags protecting them. In that

position, darkness fell and the fighting temporarily abated.[57] That

evening, with the outcome still heavily in doubt, Bouquet wrote to

General Amherst of the day's events. "Whatever our Fate may

be," he concluded, "I thought it necessary to give your Excellency

this early Information."[58] The next day, the battle resumed.

In the morning, Indians continued firing into the British

defensive position. They also made several attempts to overrun the beleaguered British army. Although the Redcoats managed to repel each attack, the growing number of wounded and killed made it evident that, eventually, the continuous assaults would overwhelm the remaining soldiers.[59]

In an effort to encourage the Indians to concentrate in the open so they could be effectively engaged and defeated by his regulars, Bouquet decided upon a bold stratagem. He ordered the center of the defensive line to retreat, and they reformed behind the hill where the attacking Indians could not see them. The remaining defenders then shifted to cover the opening. Viewing the motions of the enemy, the Indians concluded that a full-scale retreat had begun. With their hearts set on a complete rout, the Indians swarmed into the now thinly held British position. At that moment, the men reforming behind the hill swung around, hitting the unaware Indians in the flank with a devastating volley. In their confused and shocked state, the Indians could not withstand the subsequent charge by bayonet and broadsword-wielding Scots. As they broke and ran, the remaining British defenders on the hill stood up and delivered a second, devastating volley. The Redcoats then proceeded to chase the fleeing Indians for several miles. The victory cost Bouquet fifty killed and sixty wounded, but it also allowed him to reach Fort Pitt on August 10 without any serious obstructions.[60]

The Battle of Bushy Run, as it came to be called, effectively ended any serious Indian threats to the British in the Ohio country. Raiding continued, and a second, bloodless campaign under Bouquet's command was required the following year, but the victory secured the British posts. Significantly, the battle occurred almost exclusively between Indian irregulars and British regulars. Because few provincial irregulars participated, Bushy Run provides a rare glimpse at how regulars might defeat irregulars in a wilderness setting.

From the start, Bouquet's 1763 expedition differed from its predecessors in its goals. Instead of attempting to march a large force through the wilderness, with all the baggage and artillery that came with it, the colonel set out to relieve an already existing, friendly post. On June 16, Governor Hamilton of Pennsylvania received the early knowledge that, "the loss of a man at Ligonier who going out on the 14th instant to bring his horse was picked up near that place, gives Blane [commander of Fort Ligonier] with many others, reason to conjecture that Pittsburg is invested and the communication cut off."[61] Such information spurred Amherst and Bouquet into action to relieve the garrison at Fort Pitt.[62]

Moreover, in letters to those close to him Bouquet expressed an additional motive for his campaign. "I march the Day after toMorrow to the Relief of Fort Pitt," he informed Hamilton, "& hope to draw the Attention of the Enemy upon me, & by that Means be of more Service to this People."[63] To Captain Simon Ecuyer, under siege at Fort Pitt, the colonel wrote, "I shall do what I can to intice the Enemy Indians to march against me."[64] Thus, Bouquet commenced his march in the expectation, and with the hope, that he would be attacked. In such a way, he planned to both relieve the British garrisons and draw off Indian raiders from the settlements. In his mind, exposing a trained, professional army to Indian attack was far preferable to risking the fall of a post and letting the colonists of Pennsylvania fight it out with Indians on unequal terms.[65]

Finally, the expedition hinged on a sound belief that appears finally adopted by British officers. In 1756, Colonel John Armstrong attacked the village of Kittanning. The offensive operation resulted in some success, but no follow up campaigns occurred. By 1763, the understanding that defensive measures could not defeat Indians seems widely accepted. General Amherst, in a letter to Bouquet, argued, "they [colonists] may now See, that without Acting offensively, the Indians will Carry their Ravages into the Heart of the Country."[66] Even a junior officer under Bouquet's command, Captain James Robertson, noted, "that the Indians could not by an defensive plan be prevented from ravageing the frontiers."[67] Bouquet's army thus presented the offensive possibility of taking the fight directly to the Indians, or, as Bouquet expressed, inviting the Indians to attack them. In that way, the army served to both relieve the garrisons and the settlers. At the same time, it might decisively defeat the Indians.

As Bouquet gathered his army for an offensive strike, the people of Pennsylvania provided little help. In fact, they once again proved completely unable to defend themselves. "The Inhabitants, in their present Position," the colonel informed Governor Hamilton after reviewing the situation, "are utterly unable to defend their scattered Plantations."[68] Another officer concurred, informing provincial officer Colonel Edward Shippen on June 20, 1763:

> "I don't pretend to conjecture; but must take liberty to wish that the poor, scattered, defenceless inhabitants on the frontiers of this Province [Pennsylvania] were put into some posture of defence, for I can safely say, from my own knowledge, that their present situation discovers them an easy prey to their enemies."[69]

Thus, just as in 1756, Pennsylvanians could not defend themselves against Indian irregulars.

The inability, or refusal, of Pennsylvanians to defend themselves became so apparent that British officers came to resent them. "The Behavior of the Inhabitants in so Rashly throwing themselves into the power of the Indians, without the least Intention or Resolution to Defend themselves," a frustrated Bouquet wrote his superior, "is Indeed very Unaccountable."[70] Later, the colonel went further:

> "I hope that we shall be able to save that infatuated People from destruction in Spite of all their Endeavours to defeat your vigorous measures: I meet every where with the Same backwardness, even among the most exposed of the Inhabitants; and makes everything move on heavily, and is disgusting to the last degree."[71]

Eventually, the colonel's travails led him to suspect corruption among the colonials, and his disgust deepened.[72] In the end, he and other British officers concluded, "these people dont deserve and coud not much relish the honor of Shareing a Victory."[73] Thus, the British received little help from the citizens of Pennsylvania.

Much of the Pennsylvanian's inability to defend themselves stemmed from the same chronic lack of armaments that crippled the colony in 1756. Informing the governor of the situation on July 1, Bouquet noted that the settlers were "[g]enerally destitute of Arms."[74] On July 3, the colonel further emphasized the situation to Hamilton, writing that, "It would not be less Necessary to send immediately, Arms & Ammunition to be Distributed to the inhabitants to defend their Reapers."[75] Finally, Bouquet issued one final plea to the governor. "The flying Inhabitants," he wrote, "are in absolute Want of Arms & Ammunition."[76] Further to the west on the extreme frontier, British commanders in the posts at Pittsburgh, Ligonier, and Bedford found it necessary to provide firearms to local settlers as well.[77]

Despite the dire straits of the citizens of Pennsylvania, the government proved extremely slow in its reaction. British officers, including General Jeffrey Amherst, found it necessary to prod the colony into action. "I think it my indispensable duty once more," he wrote to Hamilton, "to renew my instances with you to lose no time in calling your Assembly and pressing them to enable you to raise, with the utmost despatch a body of men to be employed in the defence and protection of the frontier."[78] Despite

such admonitions, many settlers fled their homes in the absence of

provincial forces to provide defense. In fact, so slow was the

raising of provincial troops that Bouquet suggested offering

rewards to those captains that raised their companies the fastest.

With the troops finally raised by mid-July, one final surprise

awaited the colonel—Pennsylvania would not allow its troops to

accompany the regulars in their march westward.[79]

To Bouquet, the lack of provincial forces moving west

with him did not prove a deterrent. He agreed with Amherst, in

that, "[t]hey [provincials] may be made very good men, in a few

hours time, for Firing Ball, & for the Defence of a Fort Attack by

Indians, particularly as you have so many Regular Officers with

you."[80] Indeed, Pennsylvania's refusal to allow its troops to move

west allowed Bouquet to garrison the forts with the men, leaving

nearly all his regulars to march for Pittsburgh.[81] Furthermore, the

regulars sent to him by Amherst included many additional officers,

allowing him to "not entrust any post to the militia without mixing some of our men with them."[82] In such a way, Bouquet could

head west with his army hoping he had left the settlements with

adequate protection.

Bouquet did, however, realize his need for some irregulars

to march with his Redcoats. He noted:

> "Having observed on our march that the
> Highlanders lose themselves in the Woods as soon
> as they got out of the Road, and can not on that
> Account be employed as Flankers; I have
> commissioned a Person here to procure me about
> thirty Woodsmen to march with us; Their Services
> are obvious…This is very irregular in me, but the
> Circumstances render it So absolutely
> necessary."[83]

In letters to both Hamilton and Amherst, the colonel expressed this

need.[84] On June 16, he asked the general for "Ranging

Companies, composed of Hunters and Woodsmen, who may be

had on the frontiers of this Province, but particularly on those of

Maryland and Virginia; and if those Levies were under the

inspection of an officer to reject the Rabble too commonly

received."[85] To encourage such men to join, Bouquet suggested

that they be allowed additional pay for dangerous duty. To further strengthen his force, the colonel also requested a light cavalry be formed. To distinguish any Indian allies that might join, the colonel dictated that a white ribbon would be worn.[86] In reality, however, Bouquet hoped that no Indians would choose to fight with him. "I should be sorry we Should ever appear to be under the least obligation to the perfidious Cherokees," he wrote Amherst, "I would rather chuse the liberty to kill any Savage that may come in our Way, than to be perpetually doubtful whether they are Friends or Foes."[87] Although Bouquet never got his cavalry or irregulars in any large numbers, the importance he placed on such troops as support for his regulars clearly demonstrates his understanding of successful wilderness strategy. He still depended primarily on his regulars to achieve his objectives, but provincial irregulars proved necessary as essential supplements.

As Bouquet struggled to ready his force, wrangling with Pennsylvania all the way, colonists in the western posts did make contributions to the war effort. As settlers all over the countryside fled eastward, a small band garrisoned Fort Loudon and prepared it to stand against attack. At Bedford, Captain Ourry reported that local citizens appeared ready and willing to stand with his small detachment of regulars against Indian raiders. Even the more exposed inhabitants of the Ligonier area, with a bit of coercion, agreed to stay on. Some of the more skilled frontiersmen, moreover, provided essential guide, escort, and scouting services for the arriving regulars. Many of these men, among them John Proctor and Christopher Lems, had previously been sergeants in the Pennsylvania and Royal American Regiments. To augment these scouts, Fort Cumberland stripped itself of its best soldiers and sent them north.[88] Men such as these were described as "[e]xcellent Woods Men, disguised like Indians & well versed in their method of traveling & acquainted with their Haunts."[89] Despite the real contributions made by some of the higher quality colonists, settlers in the western forts, more often than not, proved frustrating to their British overseers.

While organizing the defenses of Pennsylvania, Bouquet informed Amherst that "no dependence can be had on the Militia at that Post [Fort Bedford] & Ligonier."[90] Indeed, Captain Lewis Ourry at Bedford, despite the help of fine men such as Proctor and Lems, had his hands full. "This accident so near the Town has thrown the People in to a great Consternation," he informed Bouquet, "but such is their Stupidity, they will do nothing right for their own preservation."[91] Primarily, the captain struggled to keep his wards safe within the stockade. "My greatest Difficulty," he continued to Bouquet, "is to keep my undisciplined Militia from straggling by two's & three's to their dear plantations, thereby exposing themselves to be Scalped & weakening my Garrison."[92] When actually confronted by Indians, moreover, Ourry found the militia worse than useless. On one occasion, a party of haymakers with a guard of fourteen armed men fled upon being fired at by Indians. To save them, the captain risked his limited regulars outside the stockade walls. On another occasion, a party of scouts refused Ourry's orders to pursue a raiding party[93]. So upset did the captain become, that the militia officer "and the generality of his Scouting Party, I have dismist & degraded publickly."[94] The situation at Bedford became so bad, that at the first sight of regular reinforcements, Ourry quickly dashed off a letter to his commander. "Captn. Robertson's Arrival has given me great ease," he informed Bouquet, "for my Militia was a vast fatigue to me, & I could not depend Sufficiently on them to Sleep."[95]

Although Ourry greatly appreciated the sight of regulars marching to his relief, Bouquet had intended them mainly to reinforce Fort Ligonier. On June 4, Lieutenant Blane, commanding at the post, had informed the colonel of an attack. Although the fort held out, they apparently appeared in even worse shape than Ourry at Bedford. A month after Blane's report, Bouquet dispatched Robertson's force, the party that had brought Ourry so much happiness, to Ligonier's relief. As the troops passed through Bedford, the beleaguered commander could also perceive that the relief had also only arrived in small numbers.[96] "I am not of…Opinion that 100 Men can force their Way into

Ligonier," Bouquet wrote, "as they are evidently more easily discovered, & I think a small Party with a good Guide to lead them through the Woods has a better Chance to throw themselves into the Fort."[97] To accomplish the movement into Fort Ligonier, the colonel ordered them to move with great caution, during the night, and with extremely good guides.[98] Despite the small numbers of reinforcements brought by Robertson, their arrival meant the main army could not be too far behind.

The force that Bouquet ultimately marched to Bedford and Ligonier proved well composed to undergo the severe trial it faced at Bushy Run. Perhaps the only negative it possessed was its low numbers. The fall of frontier posts elsewhere required reinforcements in those areas, and in the spring of 1763, before the Indian uprising had begun, the British military as a whole in North America had been reduced. While some units had been reduced, others found themselves entirely disbanded.[99] As a result, the British military found itself understrength at precisely the worst possible moment. Yet, in other ways, Bouquet's army proved

better prepared for a wilderness fight than a different force twice
its size might be.

Many of Bouquet's soldiers belonged to light infantry
units. While maintaining the beneficial attributes of regular
troops, light infantry soldiers had gained some understanding of
irregular methods during the Seven Years' War. Also, they
typically carried lighter equipment than the usual regular troops.
As such, they proved ideal for Bouquet's march into the
wilderness. To further their fighting skills, the colonel routinely
trained them in useful tactics.[100] "Every afternoon," noted one
Pennsylvanian, "he exercises his men in the woods and bushes in a
particular manner of his own invention, which will be of great
Service in an engagement with the Indians."[101] The units Amherst
allocated to Bouquet, moreover, possessed a disproportionate
number of officers and sergeants. In the 42nd Regiment, twenty-
nine officers and forty-two sergeants commanded only 273 men.
The high numbers would prove beneficial in maintaining order
and discipline under fire. To improve the men's firing, Bouquet

abandoned the coarse artillery powder typically used by the

military and instead collected fine hunting powder from local

traders. The powder would speed ignition of the firearms, thus

increasing accuracy. Finally, the army would be well covered

during its advance. Bouquet ordered that small parties must

silently march a mile ahead of the main column, checking every

area for concealed enemies. In addition, three flanking parties

would cover each flank at a half-mile distance. Such measures, he

hoped, would avoid a serious ambush.[102] In this condition,

Bouquet set off to relieve Fort Pitt.

On August 5, the first day of the Bushy Run battle

occurred. As an army almost entirely composed of regulars,

Bouquet fared remarkably well against his irregular foe. Like

Braddock before him, the colonel quickly rushed reinforcements

forward when the front of his column fell under attack. Here,

however, the men maintained their composure and no confusion

developed as the men joined together. Instead of standing

motionless, they then used a regular tactic—the bayonet charge—

to repeatedly dislodge their attackers from the hills. The strategy worked well as a temporary expedient, but as the Indians continuously reformed and attacked elsewhere, the supply convoy in the rear of the column eventually came under fire. The threat forced Bouquet to abandon the bayonet charges, and he ultimately ordered a defensive perimeter formed on a nearby hill. As the first day ended, and the troops discovered they had no water source, Bouquet increasingly realized he could not remain on the defensive. The colonel had survived, and might emerge victorious, if he heeded the advice he had given Captain Robertson when earlier sent to reinforce Fort Ligonier.[103] "Should the...Savages attempt to mollest you on your march," he had written Robertson, "you will charge them briskly...and not suffer the Soldiers to throw away their fire till they have routed them."[104] For Bouquet, the second day of the battle provided him with an opportunity to make good on his theory.

In a bold maneuver, the colonel withdrew the troops in the center of his defenses after the Indians had resumed the attack.

The feigned retreat encouraged the attackers to eagerly purse the withdrawing troops. In effect, Bouquet's movement served to concentrate many of the Indians into a compact body, directly in front of the British soldiers. The withdrawing troops then reformed behind the hill, and executed a swinging motion around the hill, bringing them directly into the flank of the concentrated Indians. In that way, Bouquet had not only outflanked his irregular enemy, but he had also put them in a position where volley fire and the massed ranks of bayonet and broad sword wielding British regulars could be highly effective. The results proved decisive. One volley delivered at extremely close range, followed immediately by a charge with edged weapons, sent the shattered Indian force fleeing in the opposite direction.[105] "They resolutely returned the Fire," reported Bouquet, "but could not Stand the irresistible Shock of our Men, who rushing in among them, killed many of them, and put the rest to flight."[106] Those who avoided the urge to concentrate at the outset of the apparent British retreat ultimately found themselves swept along with the precipitate withdraw of their allies. Although a small amount of sniping continued, the battled ended effectively with a resounding British victory.[107108]

For their part, the Indians had used all the known tools of irregular warfare. They had managed to surprise the British column. They attacked from multiple points throughout the woods. They made the defending troops feel surrounded. With the exception of the final, definitive charge, they had also effectively avoided frontal confrontations with the British regulars. Most accounts, moreover, cite the extreme bravery with which the Indians conducted the attack. And despite some accounts of extremely low Indian numbers at the battle, most agree that the Indians and British possessed equal numbers. Finally, evidence indicates that some Indians possessed rifled guns during the battle. This weapon, with its tremendous accuracy, would have given the Indians an advantage throughout the battle. Yet, despite all the apparent advantages held by the attackers, Bouquet secured victory.[109]

In the end, British sources attribute the victory to several factors. Some claimed the Indians had been overconfident, not expecting that "they had People to cope with that understood Bush fighting as well as themselves."[110] Indeed, the British had beaten the Indians in their own environment. However, it would be difficult to argue that Bouquet's training made his troops the equals of Indians in the woods. Instead, Bouquet stressed the importance of "the cool and steady behaviour of the Troops, who did not fire a Shot without orders."[111] Bouquet directed praise to characteristics of regular, not irregular troops. The steadiness and attention to order displayed by his troops, in the end, allowed him to conduct the difficult maneuver that resulted in victory. Bushy Run, therefore, shows how well trained, well-disciplined, and well-led regulars could overpower individualistic irregular tactics in wilderness combat.

CONCLUSION

On October 1, 1764, Colonel Henry Bouquet left Fort Pitt

at the head of an army intent on finishing the war with the Indians

in the Ohio country. On November 28, the expeditionary force

arrived back at Fort Pitt, having suffered no attacks from the

Indians. In effect, the colonel had won a bloodless victory.

Hostilities, for the most part, had ended, and European prisoners

all over Ohio returned home. After nearly ten years of conflict,

Bouquet's Muskingum Expedition displays the dominance that

regulars had established in the wilderness of the Ohio country. Of

course, the peace established by Bouquet in 1764 proved to be

short lived. Periodic violence flared up, and new conflicts

developed in the 1770s. New generations of irregular and regular

warriors forgot and relearned many of the lessons from the Seven

Years' War and Pontiac's Uprising.[1]

Looking back, many lessons readily lent themselves to

these new warriors. Washington's amateurish 1754 campaign

showed the importance of good decision-making. The string of poor decisions made by the young colonel ultimately placed his men in a hopeless situation. Moreover, the men's lack of discipline worsened the situation.

Braddock showed the need to tailor regular forces to the situation at hand. Without completely altering the form and function of regular troops, the general could have found ways to use regulars effectively in the wilderness. Standing motionless, delivering volleys at an invisible enemy clearly proved useless, but the general failed to find a way to coordinate bayonet charges to dislodge his attackers from advantageous positions and keep them off-balance. Braddock's army also demonstrated that snappy dress did not necessarily make good soldiers. Putting poorly trained men into regular uniforms and plugging them into the line did not substitute for true, professional troops.

The citizens of Pennsylvania in 1756 conclusively proved that untrained irregulars were as unable to cope with skilled irregulars than their undisciplined regular colleagues before them. In fielding thousands of men, the Pennsylvanians had been completely unable to catch up with, much less defeat, the irregulars ravaging their territory. In the end, they also managed to prove that offensive, not defensive, measures were the only possible way to defeat irregular warriors.

General John Forbes first found an effective technique to use regulars in the wilderness. By building a string of defensive works, he allowed his soldiers protection from the sneaking irregular enemies. He also avoided exposing his entire force, thus eliminating the possibility of another Braddock-style defeat. With such a method, he organized an irrepressible momentum that no irregular raiding could stop.

Of course, Colonel Henry Bouquet represents the ultimate triumph of regulars over irregulars in the wilderness. The colonel had the benefit of campaign experience and years between subsequent campaigns to digest what he had learned. Ultimately, he showed that a defensive posture did not substitute for offensive measures. By using coordinated charges, he kept the irregulars from cutting his men down like grass as had happened to

Braddock. Deception and superb leadership ultimately allowed him to capitalize on the opportunity his tactics had bought him.

In the end, all of these campaigns stress a final lesson—irregular tactics cannot be used as a blanket reasoning for success in the wilderness. Many factors contributed to each individual action's success or failure. In fact, the evidence used in the preceding chapters tends to indicate that irregulars often fared poorly against regulars, even in the wilderness. Therefore, when analyzing wilderness battles, one must be aware of several factors—whether the so-called regulars were true professionals or men recently admitted into service, and whether a leader put his men in a hopeless situation—before judging whether irregular tactics ruled supreme.

CHAPTER NOTES

Chapter 1

[1] Alfred Procter James, ed., *Writings of General John Forbes: Relating to his Service in North America* (Menasha, WI: The Collegiate Press, 1938), 238.

[2] David Dixon, *Never Come to Peace Again: Pontiac's Uprising and the Fate of the British Empire in North America* (Norman, OK, University of Oklahoma Press, 2005), 64.

[3] Michael N. McConnell, *A Country Between: The Upper Ohio Valley and Its Peoples, 1724-1774* (Lincoln, NE: University of Nebraska Press, 1992), 7-8; and Charles B. Trego, *Geography of Pennsylvania* (Philadelphia: Edward C. Biddle, 1843), 57-68.

[4] Paul A.W. Wallace, *Indian Paths of Pennsylvania* (Harrisburg, PA: Pennsylvania Historic and Museum Commission, 1965), 6.

[5] Ibid, 2. Daniel K. Richter, *Facing East From Indian Country: A Native History of Early America* (Cambridge, MA: Harvard University Press, 2001), 32.

[6] William M. Darlington, ed., *Christopher Gist's Journals with Historical, Geographical, and Ethnological Notes and Biographies of His Contemporaries* (Pittsburgh: J.R. Weldin & Co., 1893), 36.

[7] Wallace, *Indian Paths*, 2; and John Florin, *The Advance of Frontier Settlement in Pennsylvania, 1683-1850: A Geographic Interpretation* (University Park, PA: Department of Geography, The Pennsylvania State University, 1977), 28.

[8] Ibid, 28; and Alfred Procter James and Charles Morse Stotz, *Drums in the Forest: Decision at the Forks, Defense in the Wilderness* (Pittsburgh: University of Pittsburgh Press, 1958), 99.

[9] Florin, *Advance of Frontier Settlement*, 26-27; and Trego, *Geography of Pennsylvania*, 27-29.

162

---

[10] Darlington, *Christopher Gist's Journals*, 271.

[11] Stanley Pargellis, ed., *Military Affairs in North America, 1748-1765: Selected Documents from the Cumberland Papers in Windsor Castle* (Archon Books, 1969), 94.

[12] McConnell, *A Country Between*, 5.

[13] George Washington, *The Journal of Major George Washington* (Williamsburg, VA: The Colonial Williamsburg Foundation, 1959), 4.

[14] George Washington to Governor Dinwiddie, May 18, 1754, in *The Writings of George Washington*, John C. Fitzpatrick ed., http://etext.lib.virginia.edu/washington/fitzpatrick.

[15] Pargellis, *Military Affairs*, 32-33.

[16] James, *Drums in the Forest*, 98.

[17] Darlington, *Christopher Gist's Journals*, 83.

[18] Ibid, 86.

[19] George Washington to Augustine Washington, June 28, 1755, in *Writings of George Washington*, Fitzpatrick.

[20] Pargellis, *Military Affairs*, 360.

[21] Wallace, *Indian Paths*, 2; and Florin, *Advance of Frontier Settlement*, 27.

[22] George Washington to Colonel Fry, May 23, 1754, in *Writings of George Washington*, Fitzpatrick.

[23] George Washington to Governor Dinwiddie, May 18, 1754, in *Writings of George Washington*, Fitzpatrick.

[24] Richter, *Facing East*, 6; McConnell, *A Country Between*, 33; and Wallace, *Indian Paths*, 9-10.

[25] James, *Writings of General John Forbes*, 141.

[26] Pargellis, *Military Affairs*, 95.

[27] James, *Writings of General John Forbes*, 229.

[28] Pargellis, *Military Affairs*, 84.

[29] Ibid, 94.

[30] Ray Allen Billington and Martin Ridge, *Westward Expansion: A History of the American Frontier* (New York: MacMillan Publishing Co., Inc., 1982), 138; and Richter, *Facing East*, 7.

[31] Charles C. Hall, ed., *Gen. Braddock's Defeat: Contemporary Reports and Later Remembrances* (Capon Bridge, WV: The Fort Edwards Foundation, 2005), 13.

[32] Ibid, 13.

[33] Ibid, 13, 24-25; and John Grenier, *The First Way of War: American War Making on the Fronteir* (New York: Cambridge Univeristy Press, 2005), 120.

[34] Allan Greer, *The People of New France* (Toronto: University of Toronto Press, 1997), 84-85.

[35] Ibid, 78; and Armstrong Starkey, *European and Native American Warfare, 1675-1815* (Norman, OK: University of Oklahoma Press, 1998), 20.

[36] Hall, *Gen. Braddock's Defeat*, 13.

[37] Ibid, 25.

[38] *State of the British and French Colonies in North America* (New York: Johnson Reprint Company, 1967), 74.

[39] Hall, *Gen. Braddock's Defeat*, 16; Pargellis, *Military Affairs*, 162-163; and Grenier, *The First Way of War*, 120.

[40] Pargellis, *Military Affairs*, 23.

[41] *Minutes of the Provincial Council of Pennsylvania, From the Organization to the Termination of the Proprietary Government* (New York: AMS Press, 1968), 518.

[42] Robert Dinwiddie to George Washington, September 30, 1756, in *Letters to Washington and Accompanying Papers*, Stanislaus Murray Hamilton ed., http://memory.loc.gov/ammem/browse/.

[43] Florin, *Advance of Frontier Settlement*, 17-19.

[44] Hall, *Gen. Braddock's Defeat*, 4.

[45] Florin, *Advance of Frontier Settlement*, 19-20.

[46] James H. Merrel, *Into the American Woods: Negotiators on the American Frontier* (New York: W.W. Norton & Company, 1999), 22; and Pargellis, *Military Affairs in North America*, 165.

[47] John Heckewelder, *History, Manners, and Customs of the Indian Nations Who Once Inhabited Pennsylvania and the Neighboring States* (New York: Arno Press & The New York Times, 1971), 191.

[48] Merrel, *Into the American Woods*, 152.

[49] Starkey, *European and Native American Warfare*, 11.

[50] Hall, *Gen. Braddock's Defeat*, 14.

[51] *Minutes*, 404.

[52] Pargellis, *Military Affairs in North America*, 84.

[53] *State of the British and French colonies in North America* (New York: Johnson Reprint Corporation, 1967), 74.

[54] Heckewelder, *History, Manners and Customs*, 192.

[55] Ibid, 75.

[56] Archibald Loudon ed., *Loudon's Indian Narratives* (Lewisburg, PA: Wennawoods Publishing, 1996), 250.

[57] Ibid, 247.

[58] Richter, *Facing East*, 5, 7, 62; Starkey, *European and Native American Warfare*, 10, 34; Brian R. Ferguson and Neil L. Whitehead, *War in the Tribal Zone: Expanding States and Indigenous Warfare* (Santa Fe: School of

American Research Press, 1999), 19; Florin, *The Advance of Frontier Settlement*, 30; Hall, *Gen. Braddock's Defeat*, 19; and McConnell, *A Country Between*, 12, 31.

[59]Starkey, *European and Native American Warfare*, 9; T.M. Hamilton, *Colonial Frontier Guns* (Chadron, NE: The Fur Press, 1980), 20; and Alice B. Kehoe, *North American Indians: A Comprehensive Account* (Upper Saddle River, NJ: Pearson Prentice Hall, 1981), 258.

[60]Colin G. Calloway, *First Peoples: A Documentary Survey of American Indian History* (Boston: Bedford/St. Martin's, 1999), 156; Starkey, *European and Native American Warfare*, 15; Richter, *Facing East*, 64-66; Frederick E. Hoxie ed., *Encyclopedia of North American Indians: Native American History, Culture, and Life from Paleo-Indians to the Present* (Boston: Houghton Mifflin Company, 1996), 668; Gregory Evans Dowd, *A Spirited Resistance: The North American Indian Struggle for Unity, 1745-1815* (Baltimore: The Johns Hopkins University Press, 1992), 12; Janet Hubbard-Brown, *Indians of North America: The Shawnee* (New York: Chelsea House Publishers, 1995), 28; Brian Fagan, *Ancient North America: The Archaeology of a Continent* (New York: Thames and Hudson, 1991), 485; David Hurst Thomas, *Places in Time: Exploring Native North America* (New York: Oxford University Press, 2000), 182,192; Bruce G. Trigger, *The Huron: Farmers of the North* (Belmont, CA: Wadsworth Thomas Learning, 1990), 54,56; and Don Higgenbotham, "The Early American Way of War: Reconnaissance and Appraisal." *William and Mary Quarterly*. 3rd Series, 44, April 1987.

[61]David Curtis Scaggs and Larry L. Nelson eds., *The Sixty Years' War for the Great Lakes: 1754-1814* (East Lansing, MI: Michigan State University Press, 2001), 150.

[62]Heckewelder, *History, Manners, and Customs*, 216.

[63]Trigger, *The Huron*, 52; Hubbard-Brown, *Indians of North America*, 26; and Starkey, *European and Native American Warfare*, 18.

[64]Loudon, *Loudon's Indian Narratives*, 249.

[65]Pargellis, *North American Military Affairs*, 162.

[66]Heckewelder, *History, Manners, and Customs*, 177-178.

[67]Hall, *Gen. Braddock's Defeat*, 9.

166

[68]Starkey, *European and Native American Warfare*, 24.

[69]Hall, *Gen. Braddock's Defeat*, 9.

[70]S.K. Stevens, Donald H. Kent, and Autumn L. Leonard eds., *The Papers of Henry Bouquet*, 6 vols (Harrisburg, PA: Pennsylvania Historical and Museum Commission, 1951-1995), 6:304; *State of the British and French Colonies*, 70; Ian McCulloch and Timothy Todish eds., *Through So Many Dangers: The Memoirs and Adventures of Robert Kirk, Late of the Royal Highland Regiment* (Fleishmanns, NY: Purple Mountain Press, 2004), 38; Heckewelder, *History, Manners, and Customs*, 177; Loudon, *Loudon's Indian Narratives*, 242, 244, 248-249; and Starkey, *European and Native American Warfare*, 18, 21-22.

[71]James, *Writings*, 117.

[72]Starkey, *European and Native American Warfare*, 19.

[73]Loudon, *Loudon's Indian Narratives*, 241.

[74]Heckewelder, *History, Manners, and Customs*, 323.

[75]Loudon, *Loudon's Indian Narratives*, 242, 248, 290; and Starkey, *European and Native American Warfare*, 18.

[76] Pargellis, *North American Military Affairs*, 294.

[77]Ibid, 160, 295; and James, *Drums*, 89.

[78] Grenier, *The First Way*, 119, 121.

[79]Pargellis, *North American Military Affairs*, 295.

[80]Ibid, 165; and *The Pennsylvania Gazette*, March 12th, 1754.

[81]*Minutes,* 496.

[82]Greer, *The People*, 113-114.

[83]Scaggs, *The Sixty Years' War*, 47, 50; Loudon, *Loudon's Indian Narratives*, 246; and Starkey, *European and Native American Warfare*, 6, 10.

[84]Francis Jennings, *Empire of Fortune* (New York: W.W. Norton & Company, 1988), 1999; and Ferguson, *War*, 19.

[85]Pargellis, *North American Military Affairs*, 39.

[86]Ibid, 261, 296.

[87]John K. Mahon, "Anglo-American Methods of Indian Warfare, 1676-1794," *Mississippi Valley Historical Review*, 45, September 1958, 256-257, 268; Richter, *Facing East*, 71; Peter E. Russell, "Redcoats in the Wilderness: British Officers and Irregular Warfare in Europe and America, 1740 to 1760," *William and Mary Quarterly*, 3rd Series, 35, Oct. 1978, 629; and Starkey, *European and Native American Warfare*, 11, 19.

[88]Richard Brookhiser, *Founding Father, Rediscovering George Washington* (New York: The Free Press, 1996), 24.

[89]Dixon, *Never Come to Peace*, 189.

[90]Scaggs, *The Sixty Years' War*, 51; and Russell, *Redcoats*, 640.

Chapter 2

[1] George Washington in Journal, March 31st, 1754, in *Writings of George Washington*, Fitzpatrick; George Washington to Robert Dinwiddie, April 25th, 1754, in Ibid.

[2] Fred Anderson, *Crucible of War: The Seven Years' War and the Fate of Empire in British North America, 1754-1766* (New York: Vintage Books, 2000), 49; and Hall, *Gen. Braddock's Defeat*, 18.

[3] Hall, *Gen. Braddock's Defeat*, 18; *The Pennsylvania Gazette*, September 19th, 1754; Washington to Dinwiddie, May 18th, 1754, in *Writings of George Washington*, Fitzpatrick; and Washington to Dinwiddie, June 12th, 1754, in Ibid.

[4] Hall, *Gen. Braddock's Defeat*, 18; and George Washington to Robert Dinwiddie, June 3rd, 1754, in *Writings of George Washington*, Fitzpatrick.

[5] *The Pennsylvania Gazette*, September 19th, 1754.

[6] Hall, *Gen. Braddock's Defeat*, 18; George Washington to Journal, May 27th, 1754, in *Writings of George Washington*, Fitzpatrick; and George Washington to Robert Dinwiddie, May 29th, 1754.

[7] Hugh Cleland, *George Washington in the Ohio Valley* (Pittsburgh: University of Pittsburgh Press, 1955), 84. The *Pennsylvania Gazette*, June 27th, 1754, September 19th, 1754; Hall, *Gen. Braddock's Defeat*, 18-19; Anderson, *Crucible*, 55; George Washington to Robert Dinwiddie, May 29th, 1754, in *Writings of George Washington*, Fitzpatrick; George Washington to Augustine Washington, May 31st, 1754, in Ibid; and George Washington to Journal, May 27th, 1754, in Ibid.

[8] J. Martin West ed., *War for Empire in Western Pennsylvania* (Ligonier, PA: Fort Ligonier Association, 1993), 21, 23.

[9] George Washington to Robert Dinwiddie, May 29th, 1754, in *Writings of George Washington*, Fitzpatrick.

[10] *The Pennsylvania Gazette*, August 1st, 1754.

[11] McConnel, *A Country Between*, 110-111.

[12] Hall, *Gen. Braddock's Defeat*, 19-20; Robert Stobo, *Memoirs of Major Robert Stobo of the Virginia Regiment* (Pittsburgh, John S. Davidson, 1854), 87; and *The Pennsylvania Gazette*, July 25th, 1754.

[13] Hall, *Gen. Braddock's Defeat*, 19; *The Pennsylvania Gazette*, July 25th, 1754; and West, *War*, 21, 23.

[14] George Washington to Robert Dinwiddie, April 25th, 1754, in *Writings of George Washington*, Fitzpatrick.

[15] Hall, *Gen. Braddock's Defeat*, 17, 20-21; and *The Pennsylvania Gazette*, August 22nd, 1754.

[16] *The Pennsylvania Gazette*, August 1st, 1754, and August 22nd, 1754.

[17] Hall, *Gen. Braddock's Defeat*, 20.

[18] George Washington to Robert Dinwiddie, March 9th, 1754, in *Writings of George Washington*, Fitzpatrick.

[19] Ibid.

[20] Hall, *Gen. Braddock's Campaign*, 20.

[21] George Washington to Robert Dinwiddie, March 20th, 1754, in *Writings of George Washington*, Fitzpatrick.

[22] *The Pennsylvania Gazette*, August 22nd, 1754.

[23] George Washington to Robert Dinwiddie, May 18th, 1754, in *The Writings of George Washington*, Fitzpatrick; and George Washington to Robert Dinwiddie, May 9th, 1754, in Ibid.

[24] Anderson, *Crucible*, 63; *Minutes*, 182; George Washington to Journal (in note added later), March 31st, 1754, in *Writings of George Washington*, Fitzpatrick.

[25] *Minutes*, 136.

[26] *The Pennsylvania Gazette*, July 25th, 1754; and George Washington to Robert Dinwiddie, May 29th, 1754, in *Writings of George Washington*, Fitzpatrick.

[27] George Washington to Augustine Washington, May 31st, 1754, in *Writings of George Washington*, Fitzpatrick; *The Pennsylvania Gazette*, August 1st, 1754, August 22nd, 1754; Stotz, *Outposts*, 97; and Gerald K. Kelso, "Palynology in Historical Rural-Landscape Studies: Great Meadows, Pennsylvania," *American Antiquity*, Vol. 59, No. 2 (April 1994), 361.

[28] George Washington to Robert Dinwiddie, May 27th, 1754, in *Writings of George Washington*, Fitzpatrick.

[29] *The Pennsylvania Gazette*, August 1st, 1754.

Chapter 3

[1] Anderson, *Crucible*, 86.

[2] Walter Isaacson, *Benjamin Franklin: An American Life* (New York: Simon & Schuster,
2003), 108.

[3] Anderson, *Crucible*, 96; and Andrew J. Wahll ed., *Braddock Road*

Chronicles 1755 (Bowie, MD: Heritage Books, 1999), 350.

[4] Anderson, Crucible, 96-100.

[5] Ibid, 105.

[6] *Minutes*, 514.

[7] Wahll, *Braddock Road*, 358.

[8] Anderson, *Crucible*, 101.

[9] Norman K. Risjord, *Representative Americans: The Revolutionary Generation* (Lanham, MD: Rowman & Littlefield Publishers, Inc., 2001), 58; and Russell, *Redcoats*, 635.

[10] Pargellis, *North American Military Affairs*, 83.

[11] George Washington to Robert Dinwiddie, July 18th, 1755, in *Writings of George Washington*, Fitzpatrick; *The Pennsylvania Gazette*, December 19th, 1754; Stephen W. McBride, Kim Arbogast McBride, and Greg Adamson, *Frontier Forts in West Virginia: Historical and Archaeological Explorations* (Charleston, WV: West Virginia Division of Culture and History, 2003), 3.

[12] Hall, *Gen. Braddock's Defeat*, 22, 41.

[13] Wahll, *Braddock Road*, 358.

[14] *The Pennsylvania Gazette*, July 10th, 1755; and McConnell, *A Country Between*, 119.

[15] Dixon, *Never Come to Peace*, 31.

[16] Russell, *Redcoats*, 642.

[17] Pargellis, *North American Military Affairs*, 85.

[18] *The Pennsylvania Gazette*, May 22nd and 29th, 1755; Hall, *Gen. Braddock's Defeat*, 33; Wahll, *Braddock's Road*, 361; and *Minutes*, 483.

[19] George Washington to Augustine Washington, June 28th, 1755, in *Writings of George Washington*, Fitzpatrick.

[20] *The Pennsylvania Gazette*, July 24th, 1755; George Washington to Augustine Washington, June 28th, 1755, in *Writings of George Washington*, Fitzpatrick; George Washington to Robert Jackson, August 2nd, 1755, in Ibid; and Frank A. Cassell, "The Braddock Expedition of 1755: Catastrophe in the Wilderness," *Pennsylvania Legacies*, Vol. 5, No. 1, May 2005, 14.

[21] Russell, *Redcoats*, 643.

[22] Hall, *Gen. Braddock's Defeat*, 43.

[23] Wahll, *Braddock Road*, 347, 356, 367; and Hall, *Gen. Braddock's Defeat*, 33, 35.

[24] Wahll, *Braddock Road*, 354.

[25] Ibid, 352.

[26] Ibid, 368-370.

[27] Ibid, 347, 351, 358, 360-361; *Minutes*, 496, 501; Hall, *Gen. Braddock's Defeat*, 40-41; and Loudon, *Loudon's Indian Narratives*, 126.

[28] Anderson, *Crucible*, 100.

[29] Hall, *Gen. Braddock's Defeat*, 40; *Minutes*, 497; and Wahll, *Braddock Road*, 348, 354, 357-358.

[30] Wahll, *Braddock Road*, 367, 370.

[31] Ibid, 370.

[32] *Minutes*, 517.

[33] Ibid, 496, 500-501; Wahll, *Braddock Road*, 351, 356-357, 359-360, 366; Hall, *Gen. Braddock's Defeat*, 34; and Darlington, *Christopher Gist's Journals*, 267.

[34] Wahll, *Braddock Road*, 356-357.

[35] Ibid, 349.

[36] Ibid, 364-365.

[37] Hall, *Gen. Braddock's Defeat*, 38.

[38] Wahll, *Braddock Road*, 346, 352, 356, 367-369.

[39] Ibid, 346, 353-354, 356; and Hall, *Gen. Braddock's Defeat*, 34, 39-40.

[40] Darlington, *Christopher Gist's Journals*, 267-268.

[41] Hall, *Gen. Braddock's Defeat*, 36.

[42] Wahll, *Braddock Road*, 365, 367-369; and Mahon, *Anglo-American Methods*, 269.

[43] Wahll, *Braddock Road*, 350-351, 354, 358, 365; George Washington to Robert Dinwidde, July 18th, 1755, in *Writings of George Washington*, Fitzpatrick; Anderson, *Crucible*, 100; and Hall, *Gen. Braddock's Defeat*, 38.

[44] *Minutes*, 501; Hall, *Gen. Braddock's Defeat*, 34-35, 41; and Wahll, *Braddock Road*, 351, 354.

[45] Pargellis, *North American Military Affairs*, 34.

[46] Ibid, 83; *Minutes*, 498.

[47] Wahll, *Braddock Road*, 367-368.

[48] *The Pennsylvania Gazette*, December 19th, 1754.

[49] Hall, *Gen. Braddock's Retreat*, 34.

[50] Ibid, 41.

[51] Ibid, 35, 40; Wahll, *Braddock Road*, 346-347, 349-351; and Dixon, *Never Come to Peace*, 32.

[52] Wills, De Hass, *History of the Early Settlement and Indian Wars of West Virginia* (Parsons, WV: McClain Printing Company, 2000), 128.

[53] Lyman C. Draper and Ted Franklin Belue, ed., *The Life of Daniel Boone* (Mechanicsburg, PA: Stackpole Books, 1998), 132.

[54] Wahll, *Braddock Road*, 370.

[55] Hall, *Gen. Braddock's Defeat*, 22, 38; Dixon, *Never Come to Peace*, 32; *Minutes*, 480-482, 600; Wahll, 347, 350, 352, 356, 358, 361; George Washington to Robert Dinwiddie, July 18th, 1755, in *Writings of George Washington*, Fitzpatrick; George Washington to Memorandum, July 9th, 1755, in *Writings of George Washington*, Fitzpatrick; *The Pennsylvania Gazette*, August 28th, 1755.

[56] Wahll, *Braddock Road*, 353.

Chapter 4

[1] R.S. Stephenson, "Pennsylvania Provincial Soldiers in the Seven Years' War," *Pennsylvania History*, 196-198.

[2] McConnel, *A Country Between*, 71.

[3] Stephenson, *Pennsylvania*, 196-198; and Mathew C. Ward, "An Army of Servants: The Pennsylvania Regiment during the Seven Years' War," *The Pennsylvania Magazine of History & Biography*, CXIV, no. ½ (January/April 1995): 76.

[4] Thomas Lynch Montgomery, ed., *Report of the Commission to Locate the Site of the Frontier Forts of Pennsylvania*, 2 vols (Harrisburg, PA: WM Stanley Ray, State Printer, 1916), 2:72.

[5] Stephenson, *Pennsylvania*, 194.

[6] Ibid, 199; and Matthew C. Ward, *La Guerre Sauvage: The Seven Years' War on the Virginia and Pennsylvania Frontier* (Unpublished PhD Dissertation, College of William & Mary, 1992), 420-440.

[7] Montgomery, *Report*, 1:543; and *The Pennsylvania Gazette*, April 15, 1756, April 22, 1756, September 9, 1756.

[8] Montgomery, *Report*, 1:607-609, 2:451-452.

[9] *Collections of the Massachusetts Historical Society* Vol. 6, 3rd Series, (Boston: American Stationer's Company, 1837): 143; William A. Hunter,

"Victory at Kittanning," *Pennsylvania History* XXIII, no. 3 (July, 1956): 19-20; and Anderson, *Crucible*, 163.

[10] Stephenson, *Pennsylvania*, 194.

[11] *The Pennsylvania Gazette*, April 10, 1755.

[12] Ibid, May 13, 1756.

[13] Ibid.

[14] Stephenson, *Pennsylvania*, 198.

[15] Stevens, *The Papers of Henry Bouquet*, 2:35.

[16] Loudon, *Loudon's Indian Narratives*, 247.

[17] Stephenson, *Pennsylvania*, 198.

[18] Montgomery, *Report*, 1:557-558.

[19] Ibid, 2:74.

[20] Stotz, *Outposts*, 110.

[21] Montgomery, *Report*, 1:557, 576.

[22] Guy Graybill, "Fort Pomfret Castle: An Archeological Quest," *Pennsylvania Archaeologist*, 47, no. 1 (April 1977): 46.

[23] Montgomery, *Report*, 2:77.

[24] Ibid, 1:576.

[25] Stephenson, *Pennsylvania*, 202.

[26] Ibid, 203.

[27] John S. Fisher, "Colonel John Armstrong's Expedition Against Kittanning," *The Pennsylvania Magazine of History and Biography* 51 (1927): 9.

[28] Stephenson, *Pennsylvania*, 208; and Ward, *An Army*, 89.

---

[29] Ward, *An Army*, 85.

[30] *The Pennsylvania Gazette*, October 21, 1756.

[31] Montgomery, *Report*, 2:72.

[32] *The Pennsylvania Gazette*, November 20, 1756.

[33] Ibid.

[34] Ibid, March 25, 1756.

[35] Ibid, April 15, 1756, April 22, 1756, September 9, 1756; and Montgomery, *Report*, 1:543.

[36] Montgomery, *Report*, 1:607-609, 2:451-452.

[37] Hunter, *Victory*, 11-12, 23.

[38] Ibid, 14.

[39] Ibid, 13.

[40] Ibid, 12-13.

[41] Ibid.

[42] Montgomery, *Report*, 1:557.

[43] Ibid, 1:610; and *The Pennsylvania Gazette*, August 19, 1756.

[44] *The Pennsylvania Gazette*, March 25, 1756.

[45] Jennings, *Empire*, 199.

Chapter 5

[1] James, *Writings*, 70-71.

[2] West, *War*, 49.

[3] Anderson, *Crucible*, 281.

176

The Pennsylvania Gazette, September 28, 1758.

[5] Ibid, November 9, 1758.

[6] James, *Writings*, 255; and Fred Anderson, *George Washington Remembers: Reflections on the French & Indian War* (New York: Rowman & Littlefield Publishers, Inc., 2004), 23.

[7] Stevens, *The Papers*, 2:592.

[8] Ibid, 2:95.

[9] Ibid, 2:136.

[10] James, *Writings*, 102.

[11] Ibid, 108.

[12] *The Pennsylvania Gazette*, December, 21, 1758.

[13] Stevens, *The Papers*, 2:240.

[14] Montgomery, *Report*, 1:479.

[15] Ibid, 2:202.

[16] James, *Writings*, 91, 126.

[17] Ibid, 69.

[18] Montgomery, *Report*, 2:202.

[19] James, *Writings*, 191.

[20] Ibid, 192.

[21] Stevens, *The Papers*, 2:447.

[22] James, *Writings*, 168.

[23] Ibid, 118.

[24] Ibid, 77.

[25] *The Pennsylvania Gazette*, April 20, 1758, December 14, 1758.

[26] Montgomery, *Report*, 1:478.

[27] James, *Writings*, 78.

[28] Ibid, 95.

[29] Ibid, 99.

[30] Ibid, 85.

[31] Ibid, 79; and Stevens, *The Papers*, 2:258, 687.

[32] James, *Writings*, 100; and Stevens, *The Papers*, 2:124, 136, 159, 203, 402, 595.

[33] Stevens, *The Papers*, 2:240.

[34] Ibid, 2:104, 143.

[35] James, *Writings*, 116.

[36] Stevens, *The Papers*, 2:124.

[37] Ibid, 2:136.

[38] Ibid, 2:317, 349.

[39] James, *Writings*, 114.

[40] Ibid, 201.

[41] Ibid, 255; and Anderson, *Washington*, 23.

[42] Stevens, *The Papers*, 2:440-440, 473-474, 657.

[43] *The Pennsylvania Gazette*, December 14, 1758.

[44] McCulloch, *Through So Many Dangers*, 40.

[45] Ibid, 28; and *The Pennsylvania Gazette*, September 28, 1758.

[46] McCulloch, *Through So Many Dangers*, 40.

[47] Ibid, 40; *The Pennsylvania Gazette*, September 28, 1758; and Stevens, *The Papers*, 2:504.

[48] Montgomery, *Report*, 2:200-202; and Jacob L. Grimm, *Archaeological Investigations of Fort Ligonier: 1960-1965* (Pittsburgh: Annals of Carnegie Museum, 1970), 10.

[49] Montgomery, *Report*, 2:199-200.

[50] Ibid, 2:202; and *The Pennsylvania Gazette*, November 9, 1758.

[51] James, *Writings*, 229.

[52] Ibid, 238.

Chapter 6

[53] Stevens, *The Papers*, 6:4-5.

[54] Ibid, 6:6.

[55] Ibid, 6:7.

[56] Ibid, 6:326.

[57] Dixon, *Never Come to Peace*, 186-188.

[58] Stevens, *The Papers*, 6:339.

[59] Dixon, *Never Come to Peace*, 190.

[60] Ibid, 190-193.

[61] Montgomery, *Report*, 2:216.

[62] Stevens, *The Papers*, 6:327.

[63] Ibid, 6:368.

[64] Ibid, 6:328.

[65] Ibid, 6:297.

[66] Ibid, 6:314.

[67] Ibid, 6:322.

[68] Dixon, *Never Come to Peace*, 158.

[69] Montgomery, *Report*, 1:483.

[70] Stevens, *The Papers*, 6:256.

[71] Ibid, 6:326.

[72] Dixon, *Never Come to Peace*, 45-46.

[73] Stevens, *The Papers*, 6:322.

[74] Ibid, 6:280.

[75] Ibid, 6:290.

[76] Ibid, 6:308.

[77] Ibid, 6:246.

[78] Montgomery, *Report*, 1:483.

[79] Stevens, *The Papers*, 6:280, 306, 312.

[80] Ibid, 6:313.

[81] Ibid, 6:300, 315-316.

[82] Ibid, 6:295.

[83] Ibid, 6:326.

[84] Ibid, 6:279.

180

---

[85] Ibid, 6:226.

[86] Ibid, 6:248, 279-280.

[87] Ibid, 6:256.

[88] Ibid, 6:247, 271, 318, 320, 325, 328; and Montgomery, *Report*, 1:483.

[89] Dixon, *Never Come to Peace*, 145.

[90] Stevens, *The Papers*, 6:245.

[91] Ibid, 6:286.

[92] Ibid, 6:146.

[93] Ibid, 6:278, 286.

[94] Ibid, 6:286.

[95] Ibid, 6:309.

[96] Ibid, 6:217, 297.

[97] Ibid, 6:297.

[98] Ibid, 6:286, 297.

[99] Ibid, 6:186.

[100] Ibid, 6:209, 220-221, 270.

[101] Dixon, *Never Come to Peace*, 45.

[102] Ibid, 45; and Stevens, *The Papers*, 6:255, 289.

[103] *The Pennsylvania Gazette*, September 1, 1763; Stevens, *The Papers*, 6:339, 342-343; and Mahon, *Anglo-American Methods*, 270.

[104] Stevens, *The Papers*, 6:321.

[105] Ibid, 6:343; *The Pennsylvania Gazette*, September 1, 1763; and Dixon, *Never Come to Peace*, 188, 190, 193.

[106] Stevens, *The Papers*, 6:343.

[107]

[108] Ibid, 6:343; and *The Pennsylvania Gazette*, September 1, 1763.

[109] Stevens, *The Papers*, 6:227, 273, 317, 339, 342-343; *The Pennsylvania Gazette*, September 1, 1763; Dixon, *Never Come to Peace*, 190-191; and McConnell, *A Country Between*, 194.

[110] *The Pennsylvania Gazette*, September 1, 1763.

[111] Stevens, *The Papers*, 6:339.
[1] Stevens, *The Papers*, 6:14.

BIBLIOGRAPHY

PRIMARY SOURCES

MANUSCRIPTS

Hamilton, Stanislaus Murray, ed. *Letters to Washington and Accompanying Papers*. The Society of the Colonial Dames of America. http://memory.loc.gov/ammem/browse/.

BOOKS

Anderson, Fred, ed. *George Washington Remembers: Reflections on the French & Indian War*. New York: Rowman & Littlefield Publishers, Inc., 2004.

Collections of the Masschusetts Historical Society. Vol. 6, 3rd Series. Boston, American Stationers' Company, 1837.

Darlington, William M., ed. *Christopher Gist's Journals with Historical, Geographical and Ethnological Notes and Biographies of His Contemporaries*. Pittsburgh: J.R. Weldin & Co., 1893.

De Hass, Wills. *History of the Early Settlement and Indian Wars of West Virginia*. Parsons, WV: McClain Printing Company, 2000.

Draper, Lyman C. and Ted Franklin Belue, ed. *The Life of Daniel Boone*. Mechanicsburg, PA: Stackpole Books, 1998.

Fitzpatrick, John C., ed. *The Writings of George Washington.* http://etext.lib.virginia.edu/washington/fitzpatrick.

Hall, Charles C., ed. *Gen. Braddock's Defeat: Contemporary Reports and Later Remembrances*. Capon Bridge, WV: The Fort Edwards Foundation, 2005.

Heckewelder, John. *History, Manners, and Customs of the Indian Nations Who Once Inhabited Pennsylvania and the Neighboring States*. New York: Arno Press & The New York Times, 1971.

James, Alfred Proctor, ed. *Writings of General John Forbes: Relating to his Service in North America*. Menasha, WI: The Collegiate Press, 1938.

Loudon, Archibald, ed. *Loudon's Indian Narratives*. Lewisburg, PA: Wennawoods Publishing, 1996.

McCulloch, Ian and Timothy Todish, eds. *Through So Many Dangers: The Memoirs and Adventures of Robert Kirk, Late of the Royal Highland Regiment*. Fleishmanns, NY: Purple Mountain Press, 2004.

Memoirs of Major Robert Stobo of the Virginia Regiment. Pittsburgh: John S. Davidson, 1854.

Minutes of the Provincial Council of Pennsylvania, From the Organization to the Termination of the Proprietary Government. New York: AMS Press, 1968.

Pargellis, Stanley, ed. *Military Affairs in North America, 1748-1765: Selected Documents from the Cumberland Papers in Windsor Castle*. Archon Books, 1969.

State of the British and French Colonies in North America. New York: Johnson Reprint Corporation, 1967.

Stevens, S.K., Donald H. Kent, and Autumn L. Leanard, eds. *The Forbes Expedition*. Vol. 2 of *The Papers of Henry Bouquet*. Harrisburg PA: The Pennsylvania Historical and Museum Commission, 1951.

Wahll, Andrew J., ed. *Braddock Road Chronicles 1755*. Bowie, MD: Heritage Books, 1999.

Washington, George. *The Journal of Major George Washington*. Williamsburg, VA: The Colonial Williamsburg Foundation, 1959.

NEWSPAPERS

The Pennsylvania Gazette, 1748-1763.

SECONDARY SOURCES

BOOKS

Anderson, Fred. *Crucible of War: The Seven Years' War and the Fate of Empire in British North America, 1754-1766*. New York, Vintage Books, 2000.

Billington, Ray Allen and Martin Ridge. *Westward Expansion: A History of the American Frontier*. New York: MacMillan Publishing Co., Inc., 1982.

Brookhiser, Richard. *Founding Father: Rediscovering George Washington*. New York: The Free Press, 1996.

Calloway, Colin G. *First Peoples: A Documentary Survey of American Indian History*. Boston: Bedford/St. Martin's, 1999.

Dixon, David. *Never Come to Peace Again: Pontiac's Uprising and the Fate of the British Empire in North America*. Norman, OK: University of Oklahoma Press, 2005.

Dowd, Gregory Evans. *A Spirited Resistance: The North American Indian Struggle for Unity, 1745-1815*. Baltimore: The Johns Hopkins University Press, 1992.

Fagan, Brian. *Ancient North America: The Archaeology of a Continent*. New York: Thames and Hudson, 1991.

Ferguson, R. Brian and Neil L. Whitehead. *War in the Tribal Zone: Expanding States and Indigenous Warfare*. Santa Fe, NM: School of American Research Press, 1999.

Florin, John. *The Advance of Frontier Settlement in Pennsylvania, 1638-1850: A Geographic Interpretation*. University Park, PA: Department of Geography, The Pennsylvania State University, 1977.

Greer, Allan. *The People of New France*. Toronto, Canada: University of Toronto Press, 1997.

Grimm, Jacob L. *Archaeological Investigation of Fort Ligonier: 1960-1965*. Pittsburgh: Annals of Carnegie Museum, 1970.

Hamilton, T.M. *Colonial Frontier Guns*. Chadron, NE: The Fur Press, 1980.

Hoxie, Frederick E., ed. *Encyclopedia of North American Indians: Native American History, Culture, and Life from Paleo-Indians to the Present*. Boston: Houghton Mifflin Company, 1996.

Hubbard-Brown, Janet. *Indians of North America: The Shawnee*. New York: Chelsea House Publishers, 1995.

Isaacson, Walter. *Benjamin Franklin: An American Life*. New York: Simon & Schuster, 2003.

James, Alfred Proctor and Charles Morse Stotz. *Drums in the Forest: Decision at the Forks, Defense in the Wilderness*. Pittsburgh: University of Pittsburgh Press, 1958.

Jennings, Francis. *Empire of Fortune*. New York: W.W. Norton & Company, 1988.

Kehoe, Alice B. *North American Indians: A Comprehensive Account*. Upper Saddle River, NJ: Pearson Prentice Hall, 1981.

McBride, W. Stephen, Kim Arbogast McBride, and Greg Adamson. *Frontier Forts in West Virginia: Historical and Archaeological Explorations*. Charleston, WV: West Virginia Division of Culture and History, 2003.

McConnell, Michael. *A Country Between: The Upper Ohio Valley and Its Peoples, 1724-1774*. Lincoln, NE: University of Nebraska Press, 1992.

Merrell, James H. *Into the American Woods: Negotiators on the Pennsylvania Frontier*. New York: W.W. Norton & Company, 1999.

Montgomery, Thomas Lynch, ed. *Report Of The Commission To Locate The Site Of The Frontier Forts of Pennsylvania*. Harrisburg, PA: WM. Stanley, State Printer, 1916.

Richter, Daniel K. *Facing East from Indian Country: A Native History of Early America*. Cambridge, MA: Harvard University Press, 2001.

Risjord, Daniel K. *Representative Americans: The Revolutionary Generation*. Lanham, MD: Rowman & Littlefield Publishers, Inc., 2001.

Scaggs, David Curtis and Larry T. Nelson, eds. *The Sixty Years' War for the Great Lakes: 1754-1814*. East Lansing, MI: Michigan State University Press, 2001.

Starkey, Armstrong. *European and Native American Warfare, 1675-1815*. Norman, OK: University of Oklahoma Press, 1998.

Stotz, Charles Morse. *Outposts of the War for Empire: The French and English in Western Pennsylvania.* Pittsburgh: University of Pittsburgh Press, 1985.

Thomas, David Hurst. *Places in Time: Exploring Native North America.* New York: Oxford University Press, 2000.

Trego, Charles B. *Geography of Pennsylvania.* Philadelphia: Edward C. Biddle, 1843.

Trigger, Bruce G. *The Huron: Farmers of the North.* Belmont, CA: Wadsworth Thomas Learning, 1990.

Wallace, Paul A.W. *Indian Paths of Pennsylvania.* Harrisburg, PA: Pennsylvania Historic and Museum Commission, 1965.

Ward, Matthew C. *La Guerre Sauvage: The Seven Years' War on the Virginia and Pennsylvania Frontier.* Unpublished PhD Dissertation: College of William and Mary, 1992.

West, J. Martin, ed. *War for Empire in Western Pennsylvania.* U.S.A.: Fort Ligonier Association, 1993.

ARTICLES

Cassell, Frank A. "The Braddock Expedition of 1755: Catastrophe in the Wilderness," *Pennsylvania Legacies,* 5 (May 2005): 17-29.

Fisher, John S. "Colonel John Armstrong's Expedition Against Kittanning," *The Pennsylvania Magazine of History and Biography.* 51 (1927): 1-14.

Graybill, Guy. "Fort Pomfret Castle: An Archaeological Quest," *Pennsylvania Archaeologist.* 47 (April 1977): 45-58.

Higgenbotham, Don. "The Early American Way of War: Reconnaissance and Appraisal," *William and Mary Quarterly.* 3rd Series, 44 (April 1987): 230-273.

Hunter, William A. "Victory at Kittanning," *Pennsylvania History.* 23 (July 1956): 1-35.

Kelso, Gerald K. "Palynology in Historical Rural-Landscape Studies: Great Meadows, Pennsylvania," *American Antiquity*. 59 (April 1994): 359-372.

Mahon, John K. "Anglo-American Methods of Indian Warfare, 1676-1794," *Mississippi Valley Historical Review*. 45 (September 1958): 254-275.

Russell, Peter E. "Redcoats in the Wilderness: British Officers and Irregular Warfare in Europe and America, 1740 to 1760," *William and Mary Quarterly*. 3rd Series, 35 (October 1978): 629-52.

Stephenson, R.S. "Pennsylvania Provincial Soldiers," *Pennsylvania History*. 62 (Spring 1995): 196-212.

Ward, Matthew C. "An Army of Servants: The Pennsylvania Regiment During the Seven Years' War," *The Pennsylvania Magazine of History & Biography*. 119 (January-April 1995): 75-93.

INDEX

CPSIA information can be obtained
at www.ICGtesting.com
Printed in the USA
JSHW022351220322
24099JS00005B/139

9 780788 437083